MW00353663

Safe Souls

ISBN: 978-0-9961978-9-2
LCCN: 2015948379

This publication is designed to provide accurate and authoritative information with regard to the subject matter covered. It is sold with the understanding that the publisher is not engaged in rendering legal, accounting, or other professional advice. If legal advice or other expert assistance is required, the services of a competent professional should be sought. The opinions expressed by the author in this book are not endorsed by CelebrityPress® and are the sole responsibility of the author rendering the opinion.

Most CelebrityPress® titles are available at special quantity discounts for bulk purchases for sales promotions, premiums, fundraising, and educational use. Special versions or book excerpts can also be created to fit specific needs.

For more information, please write:
CelebrityPress®
520 N. Orlando Ave, #2
Winter Park, FL 32789
or call 1.877.261.4930

Visit us online at: www.CelebrityPressPublishing.com

For information on having a Safe Souls workshop at your school or place of business, please contact:
Lori Losch
5222 N 34th Place
Phoenix, AZ 85018
Or call: 1.602.820.6720
Visit us online at: www.loriliving.com/safe-souls-the-seminar

Safe Souls

TRANSFORMING RELATIONSHIPS AND BUSINESSES THROUGH THE POWER OF KIND, CLEAN AND CLEAR COMMUNICATION

By

Lori Losch

CELEBRITYPRESS®

Winter Park, Florida

CONTENTS

Testimonials 11

Acknowledgements 17

Introduction 19

Chapter 1

What is Safe Souls? 21

The Origins of Safe Souls 21

Safe Souls Keywords 25

Necker Island 26

Why is Safe Souls Important? 28

Maslow's Hierarchy of Needs 29

Fight-or-Flight 31

Kindness—The Core Message 33

Safe Souls Keywords 34

1% Milk Story 36

Safe Souls as a Spiritual Practice ...37

Chapter 2

Safe Souls Key #1: No Gossip 39

Gossip.....................................39

Gossip and Perceived Safety 41

Lord of the Flies 44

How Do We Stop the Cycle? 48

Some Just *Have* to GTC 50

Wash Your Mouth Out with SOAP..............50

What About Managing Teams? 51

The Gossiping Chefs 52

Exercise #1: GTC vs. PCH 54

Chapter 3

Safe Souls Key #2: No Triangulation 57

Recycling in Summerland 57

Ken in Las Vegas 62

Reasons We Triangulate 64

Forgiveness 65

Exercise #2: Communication and Forgiveness 66

Chapter 4

Safe Souls Key #3: No Criticism or Judgment 67

Constructive vs. Destructive Criticism 67

Judgment vs. Personal Judgment 68

A Slit for a Slut..............69

Bullied for Booze 73

Projection 75

Why Do We Judge and Criticize? 77

Exercise #3: A Transformational Game 78

Chapter 5

The Perfect Storm 81

A Trifecta 81

No One is Immune 84

Storms Don't Just Happen 85

Changing the Norm 85

Norms Gone Bad 87

Exercise #4: Cleaning Up the Past 88

Chapter 6

Tools for Transformation 91

I. Clearing Conversations 92

Realtor Joe 93

No Booze for a Yogini.....................................96

II. Committed Conversations for Action 97

The Dance of Partnership Conference 100

III. Covering People's Backs 102

Snickering Salespeople 103

You're Fired! 105

IV. Private/Public Praise 108

Corporate Love Feast 110

Change is Possible 113

Kristean Gets It 113

Exercise #5: Active Healing 115

Chapter 7

Implementation 117

The Process within an Organization 117

Assessment 118

Confidential Pre-Workshop Survey.................120

Interviewing Key Personnel 121

Pre-Workshop Session 121

Workshops 121

Observation 122

Post-Workshop 123

Safe Souls Zone 124

Organic Transformation 125

Chapter 8

We Are One 127

The Two Universal Rules: Golden and Silver 129

Christianity 130

Islam 131

Buddhism 132

Hinduism 133

Taoism 134

Shinto 135

Sikhism 136

Judaism 137

Gross National Happiness 138

Modern Day Philosophical Leaders 139

Chapter 9

Achieving Safe Souls Personally 143

The Fourth Dimension 143

The Fifth Dimension 146

Burning Man 148

Exercise #6: Seven-Day Positivity Challenge 152

Ten Actionable Steps for Creating Safe Souls 153

TESTIMONIALS

"Thank you so much for Safe Souls, Lori. The message is great wisdom and I feel it has raised my personal and business awareness to be a better leader."

~ Joe Polish, *Creator of the Genius Network® Interview Series, Founder of Genius Network®, and Co-founder of 10XTalk.com and ILoveMarketing.com, two highly popular free podcasts on iTunes.*

"The interesting thing about Safe Souls is it's one of the only topics that touches every human being. It's a very fundamental distinction and impacts every age group—young children in the sand box, grade schoolers, teenagers, teachers, business people, family members and every relationship in-between. I've never seen a topic that has as much meat on the bone and can cover as many human beings as Safe Souls.

"There's an amazing quote from Dan Sullivan that says, 'You get paid a lot more when you offer a transformation than when you offer a transaction.' Lori Losch's Safe Souls is transformational. It's one of the top three distinctions I've learned in my life. No gossip. No triangulation. No criticism or personal judgment. *Assessing others on performance, but not personally judging people* has been the most exponential and game-changing distinction that we've added through our business and our whole lives. It's powerful. It's impactful. It provides foundationally for deep, empowering relationships. Lori, thank you so much."

~ Ken Losch, *Founder and CEO, Advanced Green Innovations and Trillium Residential*

"I am an international speaker and author. I have a talk called, *Flip Your Flaws*. Obviously, the subject of flaws can be a very intimidating one for people, because we normally try to hide our flaws, which actually creates more shame. And it's my personal message that sharing actually helps to alleviate shame. So when I heard about Lori's mission and movement with Safe Souls, the whole concept deeply resonated with me. I believe that safety is the important missing ingredient for true healing and transformation. So Lori, I really give you kudos for this program that you've created, and I looked forward for corporations and individuals to be able to learn this practice, and more importantly, start putting this practice into actual reality. Thank you so much."

> ~ Renee Airya, *Award Winning Speaker, Coach,*
> *and Author,* Flip Your Flaws

"Lori Losch was kind enough to bring a distinction to me the other day, Safe Souls. I realize that I was out of integrity and inauthentic about who I was being and how I was showing up in my life. I've recently started gossiping about a certain situation. It really isn't what I stand for. It's not me. But I got into that habit of having those gossip-making conversations and even listening to gossip. That's not normally who I am. So having that awareness and bringing that distinction right in front of me, and knowing that that's not what I am or who I am, brought that awareness to me so that I could take action. So, Lori, I love your technology. I thank you for bringing that awareness to me and please spread the word."

> ~ Anil Gupta, *Speaker, Coach, and Best Selling Author,*
> Immediate Happiness

"Lori's Safe Souls has done something extraordinary, by simply and systematically tapping into the power of appreciation and kindness. These two powerhouse energetics can be accessed from anytime, anywhere...and the kicker is they are WAY more powerful than triangulation, gossip, and undercutting other people. It's this little secret that most people don't know, because we are not taught this way. Lori shows you exactly how to tap yourself into that infinite power source and, once you are in, you will be hooked and nothing else will satisfy you. It will not matter what anyone else is or is not doing or saying. You will have a refuge in your true Self at all times, that has practical, everyday applications for a higher quality of life than you ever dreamed. Stop playing small! Get big, get safe, get kind! It's useful in every single area of your life."

~ Stacie R. Cole, *Digital Marketing Director and Strategist*

"Lori, your Safe Souls philosophy and corporate workshop is timely, powerful and filling a huge void in terms of interpersonal business communication to help build, bond and catapult teams to the next level. Hands down one of the most powerful and bonding things we've done as an organization. Thank you Lori for your presence and sharing your gift of Safe Souls with us."

~ Maria Hernandez-Carter, *Author and Founder,* This One Life

"I had the chance to be part of Lori Losch's Safe Souls seminar this past year. I really enjoyed her enthusiasm about the subject. She makes excellent points about triangulation within an organization. I believe I have been guilty of this myself. I also really enjoyed the public praise exercise, which was eye opening for me. I really did not have a good handle on how I was being perceived by my business associates. Even though I have my own company, I love the people I work with outside of it and this seminar helped me to become even closer to them."

~ Carolyn Boroden, *Technical Analyst of Stocks and ETFs and Founder of Synchronicity Market Timing. Carolyn, who is also known as The Fibonacci Queen, is a recurring guest on CNBC's Mad Money.*

"For me personally, working in a safe environment or 'being safe' is a transformational concept. Why? Because when I feel safe I do not waste time or energy worrying about failure. I plan for setbacks, but not failure. I also do not worry about others exploiting my personal weaknesses in a negative way. When I feel safe I have a calmness of soul and a clarity of thought that allows me to see what needs to be done and imagine what is possible. Being safe frees me to act in a proactive and productive manner. I am able to accomplish and help others accomplish what was previously thought not possible.

"Being safe requires that I first act as a safe person. I provide to others a safe place to think, plan and work. I protect them and act in a manner to help them succeed. Next, I must have the faith to trust that others will provide a safe place for me. Now that I have experienced what a safe place is through Safe Souls being implemented at my company, I choose to live in this environment. It is where I feel peace and where I experience miracles."

~ Mark Killpack, *Senior VP at BOKF Equipment Finance*

"I'm so grateful for Lori, and what she's been doing with Safe Souls. Safe Souls gives me a way to measure the people I surround myself with every day. It also allows me to be accountable for my thoughts, my words and my actions, because I know that God is always watching, knows what I'm thinking about and knows what I say and what I do, 24/7. I'm so grateful for Lori and what she's been creating and sharing. I look forward to Safe Souls being of service to so many people.

"I practice Safe Souls every moment. Specifically, on a spiritual level with how I think. I'm very in tune with my body, so thinking positively with loving thoughts about others and myself is really important. If I catch myself thinking a thought that's not in line with who I want to be, I correct it. I change it to being a loving and compassionate thought rather than a critical or judgmental one. This is Safe Souls. It allows me to really engage with a person lovingly. Even in conversation I think people feel that love. It's that mutual feeling of love between people in conversation and being completely in sync with that person, that's awesome. Because if God has put that person in front of you, then that person is there for a reason and we're meant to listen to them. They are a reflection of ourselves as well. So I think Safe Souls has been amazing to that end.

"It also helps me pay attention to small details, as little things do matter. Even if I don't think something is a big deal, it might be to somebody else. I think that's what happens in the world— we just keep living our lives and unintentionally make mistakes, which affect other people on a big level. The decisions of one person immediately affect another person because everything's interconnected. Safe Souls is an amazing thing because we can all learn to be Safe Souls by focusing on our own soul and, through love and compassion, we can make it safe for other people as well. That in turn will make this world a better place."

~ Michael Tree, *Dartmouth Graduate*

"I wanted to talk a little about Safe Souls and how it made me a better team member. One of the biggest things that stuck out for me with Safe Souls was the fact that it was designed to eliminate negative energy at the source. And that negative energy could transform into anything from a decrease in confidence to a lower productivity output. It can also cause discomfort in your environment, and eventually, you won't want to be in that environment anymore, and that's not good.

"One place I practice Safe Souls is in the work I do, which is video. I need feedback and, before Safe Souls, I never really received any. It was just: Do it, get it done, and it's done. I was concerned that maybe my work wasn't good enough, but at the same time, I was still employed. I was not clear on the quality of the product or if they liked the videos that I created. We do quarterly meetings and we do daily meetings, but they're bigger-picture meetings. I wanted to wait until the quarterly meetings to bring everything to the table and say, 'Hey, you know, I would appreciate feedback. I'm not asking for a big cheer and pat on the back. I just want feedback. Is my work good? Is it bad? Is there anything I could change? Can *I* change?'

"Safe Souls teaches to not gossip or triangulate so I was straight, and asked for what I needed—feedback. After just bringing that up front, just that minor detail, I noticed that my team members were more prone to approach me and say, 'Hey, I like this. Can you change that?' Or, 'Hey, that was great. I loved it.' Just that little experience alone gives me a lot of confidence when I walk into the office. I feel confident, like, 'Okay, I know what I'm supposed to do and I'm doing it right. And no one is talking behind my back about it.' It just makes me an overall happier person, in a sense. So that's what Safe Souls has done for me.

"It's one of the greatest things to pop up in the $25K meeting and we applied it to our culture in Piranha Marketing immediately. So, yeah, I definitely appreciate it. Like I said, it's good for your personal life, work life, and it just makes things easier for me. That's Safe Souls, what it's done for me, and what it could possibly do for you. Thank you."

~ Rahkeem Kearney, *Multi-media, Piranha Marketing*

ACKNOWLEDGEMENTS

One of my greatest life lessons is understanding and embracing the fact that we never accomplish anything significant by ourselves. Even physical adventures like summiting Mount Kilimanjaro or trekking to Everest Base Camp seemed to be personal accomplishments, but they were not. They were communal. Local sherpas carried our extra gear, experienced guides led the way, talented cooks created nourishment, and fellow trekkers provided laughter and companionship. It has been the same in creating and writing Safe Souls. This has been a team effort and one that without certain GUS (God/Universe/Spirit) directed synchronicities, would never have happened.

Thank you firstly to Ken, my beloved, for embracing Safe Souls and encouraging me to speak out about this way of operating. You have been my head cheerleader and have inspired me to put Safe Souls into a formula that can be shared with many. I saw the following sign recently:

> **The Creative Process**
> 1. This is awesome.
> 2. This is tricky.
> 3. This is crap.
> 4. I am crap.
> 5. This might be ok.
> 6. This is awesome.

When I would get stuck on number 3 or 4, you would always take my hand and lead me to number 6. Deep gratitude.

Thank you, mom, for who you are. Without even realizing it, you planted the Safe Soul seed within me at a very young age.

You have continued to demonstrate what it is to be a kind soul and I love you for that!

Thank you, John Carter, for inviting me to give my first Safe Souls workshop to your leadership team. That workshop was the impetus for getting Safe Souls out of my head and down on paper. Thanks for believing in me!

Thank you to my publisher, Celebrity Press, for helping me create this beautiful book. Your team has been fantastic to work with and I'm forever grateful. A deep bow to you all.

Thank you to those who have adopted the Safe Souls lifestyle and have encouraged others to do the same. Change happens one person at a time and I'm grateful for the Safe Soul train chugging along, growing in numbers, and being a stand for kind, clean, and clear communication.

I especially thank all the people who have been *unsafe* souls to me. If it weren't for you, I would never have developed this concept. As humans, if we had never experienced the chill of a winter's night, we would never have created fire. Similarly, if I had not felt unsafe in so many instances, I would not have created Safe Souls. So to you, I'm grateful.

Lastly, thank you for reading this short book. I hope it effects positive change in your life and in the lives of those you touch. Love is the way and the following concepts are guideposts leading in that direction.

INTRODUCTION

As children, we have many keepers of our souls—parents, teachers, babysitters, and perhaps older siblings. They help us navigate the waters of life and try to keep our little soul beings safe. Sometimes they do a great job and sometimes they don't, and we wind up with all sorts of soul wounds and psyche scars.

As adults, we can look back, forgive, and move on. We can understand that all life experiences are part of our growth and development. We can even be thankful for the tough experiences over which we had little or no control, because we can see that they made us the great people we are today. With age comes wisdom and the responsibility to be the keepers of our own souls.

Throughout life, we may encounter unsafe physical situations such as bullying, domestic violence, or abuse. These situations are easy to identify and most of us proactively find safe havens for our bodies. But what about the responsibility we have for our more subtle emotional, mental, and even spiritual safety? Emotional, mental, and spiritual abuse can be soul suicide, producing serious wounds and scars that often last a lifetime. Avoiding this—both within ourselves and toward others—is the topic of Safe Souls.

What if we could create a world where—when we attended school, showed up for band practice, arrived at a business meeting, or simply went home for dinner—we always knew our tribe had our backs covered? That our souls were safe? Being employed and feeling safe do not have to be mutually exclusive— you can be safe, happy, and employed. Being a member of a school system or volunteer organization or family doesn't have to be synonymous with having to navigate soul-destroying land mines. In fact, it is your right to be safe—but, as an adult, your soul's safety rests securely in your hands. You have a choice as to what you allow into your 'soul space' and you also have the power to influence everyone around you. You can either create fear, pain and trauma or safety, ease and harmony.

"Research shows that exclusion [and I would say exclusion likely makes a person feel unsafe amid his peers] triggers activity in the same part of the brain that controls physical pain," says Judith V. Jordan, Ph.D., an assistant professor of psychiatry at Harvard Medical School. "For some, rejection from a friend group can be more painful than being rejected by a crush."

Wouldn't it be freeing to arrive at the office on Monday morning without your pain centers activated? Wouldn't having friends and family members who are dedicated to your soul's safety be empowering? Wouldn't it feel wonderful to be known as someone who stands for other's souls? Not only is it possible—it is relatively simple to create such a haven. Read on and you'll see how.

CHAPTER 1

WHAT IS SAFE SOULS?

*I've learned that people will forget what you said,
people will forget what you did, but people
will never forget how you made them feel.*

~ Maya Angelou

THE ORIGINS OF SAFE SOULS

My mom taught me my first lesson on how to be a Safe Soul. She would not have defined it as such, but she was the embodiment of the saying: *If you don't have anything nice to say, don't say anything at all.* She didn't tolerate negative words, gossip, triangulation, or criticism. I might come home from school and complain, "My teacher did this and that and was so unfair!" My mom would invariably say, "Let's take a step back. Did you do something to provoke that?" Or, "What might be going on in his world to cause that sort of mood?" While these cross examinations drove me crazy—I was likely just looking for someone to co-sign my crappy attitude—I did learn to approach conflict and challenges from a different perspective. I started seeing people with compassion rather than criticism.

As I grew into teenhood and later into adulthood, approaching others without judgment and with compassion was the standard by which I strove to live. I was elated when a high school classmate recently stopped me on the seawall. He was excited to see me after many years and said, "Lori! Do you know that you were the only one who was nice to me at Sentinel when I arrived from Iran?" He described how that transformed his high school experience

21

and gave him hope. He said that this simple act of compassion, kindness, and acceptance changed things dramatically for him. His words were sweet honey to my soul and reminded me of Maya Angelou's quote at the beginning of this chapter.

I don't share that story for my own gain; I share it to highlight how impactful our kindness can be, especially if something troublesome is going on in another person's life. I had no clue that my attitude towards Farhad was a refreshing oasis in his otherwise unfortunate high school transition.

I was a little naïve, however, to believe the entire world worked that way and I encountered a number of situations where my philosophy was not reciprocated. Some did not have my or other's best interests in mind. Backs were often not covered. Loyalty was not always honored. But I didn't have the tools back then to really evoke change, so my response was to avoid those that seemed unkind or unsafe. I withdrew, often silently. Many times I just retreated into my shell, as it seemed like the only truly safe haven. I began to see a pattern emerge as to what being safe, or not, meant. But to my young eyes, it wasn't quite in focus yet.

As I grew out of early adulthood, I began to realize that I could in fact be a catalyst for change. I learned to speak up. People did not always realize they were being critical, judgmental, or that their gossip had such a negative and hurtful impact on others. When I encountered these situations I began to gently suggest there was a different, more empowering, way of thinking, speaking, and treating people. I offered my view on operating as a Safe Soul—I'll define this shortly—and many people listened and committed to acting differently. And many did not. Others took time. One such person was my future husband.

When we met in 2008 and I subsequently started visiting him in Phoenix, I was thrown into a scene that had me feel very uneasy. While there were periods of fun and laughter, there was an underlying theme of conflict within his family—mainly between him, his kids, and his siblings, but also among extended family members. There was much dissention and fighting and some of them could not be in the same room with each other. Some had not seen each other for years. There were clearly many souls feeling unsafe in the family. Some still are.

But he refused to admit that the way they were relating to each other was toxic and harmful. He didn't see the connection between the micro-strife and the macro-brokenness—the small nuances that were creating major conflicts. When I shared the Safe Souls distinction, he said, "You're just being an overly sensitive woman," and, "This is how guys talk and kibitz with each other."

However, I pressed. "Ken, I feel really unsafe in your household. The fighting and gossiping is causing a constant state of cortisol-induced stress. What you're all doing is so harmful. No wonder no one seems to get along very well long-term. No one is being genuine with any level of consistency. One person will come up all nice to the other to his face and then turn around and say, 'He's such an idiot!' behind his back."

I have always been empathic, intuitive, and can strongly sense the emotions of those around me, so the abundance of negativity literally made me feel sick and nervous. So I did my best to create change. More on that later.

Parts of my husband's work environment were equally toxic. He ran a large organization—at the time he had several hundred employees—and a few of the executives felt super unsafe. After sitting through some meetings with them, I couldn't help but notice how much some of the leadership gossiped about others and how critical they could be. Cutting people down was just a part of their normal conversation. They all seemed to be outwardly charming people, so the critical ethos had likely just slipped in innocently. I think this is often the human default condition.

The boardroom had a fantastic street view. You could clearly see all the lovely, colorful, and eclectic people that lived and worked in Tempe, Arizona, many of them students at ASU. A few of the team members would sit in the boardroom and make comments about the passersby like, "Wow, look at the size of her ass." Or, "What a ridiculous outfit." Or, "That guy's clearly trying to be too cool for school."

I thought to myself—why are these well-educated, successful, and generally kind people being so negative and critical? At the time, my husband did not understand or agree with my perceptions. When I asked him about the banter, he said, "You're just being supersensitive again. This is how guys act."

"Not in my world," I said.

Everything I have learned about aspiring towards kindness, refraining from criticism, and avoiding negative speaking is embedded in my mind and heart, and I simply could not accept what was happening.

After unsuccessfully trying to change things—both at home and at the office—I finally gave up and said, "I can't be in this environment anymore. I love you, but I'm moving out." I explained that I'm too committed to my soul's wellbeing to put it in harm's way any longer. He didn't fully understand, but my leaving had him take notice. He wanted me back in his home so he was thrust into a situation where he had to listen, reflect on the truth of my observations, and consider my stand.

Then the proverbial penny dropped.

He said, "I didn't even know why I did it, but when I would leave the boardroom for a bio break, there was something in me that had me go really quickly so I could be back in the boardroom ASAP. I didn't even realize it or have the words for it, but now I know that my soul wasn't feeling safe. If they're doing that behavior behind everyone else's back, of course, they're also doing it behind mine." He immediately understood the premise that if people are fundamentally gossipers or criticizers, that's who they are. If they are gossiping about other people behind their backs, they are going to be gossiping behind his back, too. I believe past behavior predicts future behavior and, unless there is a radical new commitment to being the keeper of other's souls, many people will just not change. We avoid those people as best we can.

SAFE SOULS KEYWORDS

Safe: *not able or likely to be hurt or harmed in any way; not in danger.*

Soul: *the principle of life, feeling, thought, and action in humans; the spiritual part of humans as distinct from the physical part; the emotional part of human nature.*

According to Harvard Professor and bestselling author Shawn Achor, "Our soul is the very essence of our being that causes us to feel joy and connect with other people."

John Mackey, Co-Founder and Co-CEO of Whole Foods says, "The soul is the deepest inner part of our being where the essence of who we are exists."

Soul Researcher and author Gary Zukav believes, "The soul is the highest, most noble part of ourselves that we can reach for."

Speaker, author and TV personality Iyanala Vanzant says, "The soul is the fingerprint of God that becomes a physical body."

I define a **Safe Soul** in two ways:

1. *the feeling you have when you know your back is fully covered by your tribe.*

2. *a person who lives the Safe Souls distinction, thus fosters Safe Souls in others. The Safe Souls distinction calls for: No Gossip, No Triangulation, and No Criticism. It's that simple.*

Now that my husband sees, understands, and has embraced the Safe Souls formula, he says, "You were the canary in the coal mine. We didn't even realize we were being so harmful to each other."

He immediately implemented Safe Souls in his business, at home, and socially. Now he runs two organizations with about 160 team members—property managers, project managers, accountants, inventors, engineers, lawyers, etc.—and he has implemented Safe Souls in both environments. It has made a massive difference, not only internally, but also in how they do business with others.

Ken approached me not too long after he began implementing Safe Souls and said, "Lori, this is so powerful! I've done hundreds of millions of dollars worth of real estate deals and nobody has ever before sent me a check without a signed contract, but now with Safe Souls in operation, I've got investors sending me quarter million dollar checks on a handshake. They intuitively know that if I'm operating with this level of integrity in my speech, in my thinking, and in my being, that I'm operating with the same level of integrity in my business."

> *According to Ken, Safe Souls is the single most effective business strategy he has encountered and implemented in his 35+ years of being an entrepreneur.*

It was very exciting to see Safe Souls grow within his organizations. Now, some people are simply incapable of operating within the confines of not gossiping, triangulating, or criticizing others, and those few people have found employment elsewhere...with our blessing.

NECKER ISLAND

I recently had the privilege of spending time with Sir Richard Branson on Necker Island, his gorgeous private oasis in the British Virgin Islands. Various events took place throughout the week—kite surfing, tennis tournaments, business mastermind sessions, theme parties, and more. About twenty-five people were invited to the week-long event, representing about fifteen different companies.

During one of the mastermind sessions, each company's leader was asked to present a ten-minute TED-style talk. The topic?

An idea that has added at least a quarter million dollars to your organization's bottom line.

The talks were varied. Some were technical, some were about systems and procedures, some were about environmental concerns, some were about marketing. Then it was Ken's turn. He asked me if he could share Safe Souls.

"Of course!"

I loved that a gathering of international and influential business leaders would be hearing about Safe Souls. It has significantly impacted my life, has wildly benefitted Ken's companies, and has been transformational in our personal relationships, so we'd love for the Safe Souls movement to go global. The world needs more kindness and this formula, coupled with these people, has the power to usher it in.

Ken began, "Let me tell you about a game changer for our company called Safe Souls. My wife developed it and I'm sharing it with you because it works...and it has added *at least* a quarter million dollars to our company's bottom line." He went into detail about how Safe Souls has impacted him both personally and professionally.

After the talk, one of the other participants, a man who owns an options trading and training company, asked if I would be willing to come and facilitate a day-long workshop for him and his organization's leaders. They were having their annual retreat in the Grand Cayman Islands that July and Safe Souls was just what he felt his company needed. I happily—with some fear and trepidation peppered in—accepted the invitation and immediately got busy creating my first Safe Souls workshop. It was a six-hour event and extremely transformational. In fact, one of the participants said it was the single most impactful thing they'd done together as an organization. My heart swelled. Many guests also encouraged me to put the workshop information into a book so they could share it with their family and friends.

The seeds were planted and this book is the fruit of those seeds.

WHY IS SAFE SOULS IMPORTANT?

I can often perceive when others are feeling unsafe and I have felt unsafe many times myself. This happens when I don't sense that someone has my best interest at heart—when their words and actions are different to my face than they are behind my back. (People's 'private' opinions almost always get back to us and we can usually simply sense their malice.)

In the workplace, this lack of perceived safety can send people into a fight-or-flight mode, thus decreasing their creativity, productivity, happiness, and ultimately the company's bottom line. In an unsafe environment, people aren't free to be who they are. They aren't free to flourish. We need to trust that if someone has an issue with us they will address it directly, rather than going to a colleague to air their opinions.

Toxic communication is extremely damaging to people and to companies, therefore, implementing Safe Souls is critically important. Not only does it optimize employee morale and effectiveness, it can also increase an organization's profitability. If an organization shares its stand for Safe Souls among its partners, suppliers, investors, and customers, they will all know they are dealing with a company highly committed to integrity.

This changes everything.

There are countless studies on happiness and productivity in the workplace, indicating how both are increased when people feel empowered to be themselves. Dr. Tim Hallet, a sociologist at

Indiana University, conducted one such study about the negative impact of gossip. In a *New York Times* article, *Can You Believe How Mean Office Gossip Can Be?* he states, "Office gossip can be a form of reputational warfare. It's like informal gossip, but it's richer and more elaborate. There are more layers to it because people practice indirectness and avoidance. People are more cautious because they know they can lose not just a friendship, but a job."

An overtly hostile environment is not always the culprit. In my husband's real estate development company, it was more subtle. Ken said, "Once I really understood Safe Souls, I got in touch with a strange and underlying feeling—I didn't want to leave the room during a meeting, because when I did, I felt uneasy. What were they going to say behind my back after I had just listened to them criticize a bunch of other people behind their backs? I was trying to be creative and put the best possible product out to the market, but part of my spirit and part of my soul was in protective mode. I just couldn't clearly see the damage that had been occurring."

MASLOW'S HIERARCHY OF NEEDS

Abraham Maslow was a 20th century American psychologist who developed a theory or hierarchy of needs, based on the notion that humans fulfill our needs in order of priority. It begins with our basic physiological needs and culminates in self-actualization.

Professor David Livermore, of the Cultural Intelligence Center, teaches a course called, *Customs of the World: Using Cultural Intelligence to Adapt, Wherever You Are.* In this course, he explains that societies are based on either Individualism or Collectivism philosophies. If Maslow had lived in a more collective society, he would have likely substituted 'social harmony' for 'self-actualization' and placed it at the top of the pyramid.

Either option—self-actualization or social harmony—is virtually impossible if our individual needs are not met at the lower levels of the triangle. Maslow placed safety just above physiological needs but under, love, esteem, and self-actualization (or social harmony). This means that if we do not first feel safe, the attributes above safety cannot be fully realized. If we do not feel safe, suffering ensues and growth is thwarted. Therefore, safety is not a want— we don't just *want* to feel safe. We *need* to feel safe.

Maslow's Hierarchy of Needs

Higher up the pyramid in self-actualization (or social harmony if you are from a more collective culture), important aspects such as creativity and problem solving are activated more acutely. If a person is stuck at the level of safety, these higher needs are not even on the radar. In a work environment, this can hinder productivity and ultimately the growth of a company. In a family system, stagnation and separation might ensue. In the schoolyard, we often see kids giving up on their dreams, becoming bullies themselves, and generally going wayward.

People who do not feel safe will suffer in the esteem level, will lack confidence, and will not be able to achieve to their maximum potential. In the workplace, this not only hinders productivity, it can also lead to a high rate of staff turnover. The cost of hiring and training new employees unnecessarily can be enormous. If people don't feel safe amid their colleagues, within their group of friends, or among their family members, dissension will inevitably arise.

This is why implementing Safe Souls is so powerful—it can significantly increase your company's effectiveness and profitability and can radically transform your friendships and familial relationships. People will be able to self-actualize and social harmony will flourish.

FIGHT-OR-FLIGHT

The human brain is a product of millions of years of conditioning. The back of your brain houses the parts that regulate breathing, heart rate, and other essential bodily functions. As you move toward the forebrain, the functions become more complex— sight, sound, speech, movement, etc. Through millennia of development, our frontal lobe—the area of the brain that regulates thought and reasoning—has actually grown in size, however, we still have some primal parts that affect our body, thoughts, and actions.

Fear and anxiety, for example, are feelings to which our brain will react, but cannot distinguish as being a real physical threat or merely a perceived psychological one. Our ancestors had many things in nature to worry about—particularly predators! To avoid becoming an animal's dinner, our brains developed a mechanism called the fight-or-flight response. As a result, even though most of us do not have to worry about a lion or mammoth attack anymore, when we perceive a threat to our wellbeing, something happens to our brains and bodies and we kick into high alert.

Our autonomic nervous system—the part of our brain that regulates digestion, heart rate, urination, sexual arousal, pupillary response, and respiration—is broken into two separate parts: the sympathetic and the parasympathetic nervous systems. When we experience a threat, our sympathetic nervous system releases a host of chemicals and hormones into our bodies. One of these hormones, cortisol, increases our blood pressure and blood sugar, and suppresses our immune system. This gives us a boost of energy either to fight off the threat or to run like hell (fight-or-flight). We literally become supercharged for a few moments—we get stronger and faster.

Our breath quickens and our heartbeat speeds up, pumping more oxygen through our bodies. The energy usually reserved for digestion gets diverted because our muscles need that energy to either fight or run. The blood vessels will constrict in certain parts of the body and will dilate in others. Oxygen and energy-rich blood are poured like Red Bull® into our muscles, creating readiness for us to either slay a rattlesnake or flee a lion. Our tears dry up and our pupils dilate. The bladder relaxes, our sense of hearing dulls, and we experience tunnel vision. In some cases, our bodies may begin to shake.

This instinctual and instantaneous bodily phenomenon was fantastic for fighting off lions, but not for dealing with unsafe friends, family members, or teammates. Getting a rush of cortisol on a Monday morning while walking into work is a recipe for a heart attack. In fact, research has shown there are a disproportionate number of heart attacks on Monday mornings, especially for middle-aged males, and this has been linked to the stress associated with going back to work after the weekend. If people felt their vocational tribe had their back and that they were loved and fully supported, my guess is that this statistic would drastically improve.

While our parasympathetic systems do release hormones and chemicals to stop the fight-or-flight response and bring the body back to a state of equilibrium, this continual fluctuation can lead to heart problems, psychological illnesses, sleep disruption, digestion issues, eating disorders, and even diabetes.

Here's the fundamental thing to remember: your body cannot distinguish a lion attack from malicious gossip and criticism. A stressor or threat is one and the same to your nervous system. When you work or live in an environment full of stress, distrust, and worry, your fight-or-flight switch is constantly flickering. The parasympathetic system has to work overtime to equalize your body. Also, the body's immune system becomes depressed while in the fight-or-flight mode so you are more likely to contract an illness in that state. It is simply not healthy for your physical and mental wellbeing to be in an environment that has not adopted the Safe Souls formula. To your bodily systems, being around gossip, triangulation, and criticism is akin to being dumped into a crocodile pit at the local zoo.

Safe Souls is good for the mind, body, and spirit. It provides people with an operating manual for how specifically to treat each other with kindness and respect. A Safe Souls environment reduces stress, can improve your health and mental state, and increases productivity, creativity, and self-esteem. Self-actualization and social harmony are by-products of this healthy environment.

KINDNESS—THE CORE MESSAGE

I love the original Safe Souls workshop's tagline: *Transforming Relationships Through the Power of Kindness*, as this is the essence of Safe Souls. If simple kindness was demonstrated, the world would be a much better place. But just as there's no real efficacy in telling dieters, "Okay, go and eat more healthily," we cannot just say to others, "Be kind." Most humans need a 'How To' manual. We need specifics.

In order to remove any ambiguity around how to be kind and what it means to be a Safe Soul for others, the basic formula is simple.

1. No Gossip
2. No Triangulation
3. No Criticism

The acronym 'No GTC' easily reminds us of these concepts, as gossip, triangulation, and criticism are three fundamental ways people step out of kindness for one another. While on the surface, these behaviors may seem innocuous, they are extremely damaging. They erode confidence, trust, respect, loyalty, creativity, and productivity. The declaration and avoidance of these three domains cultivates Safe Souls.

SAFE SOULS KEYWORDS

Gossip: *information about the behavior and personal lives of other people; casual or unconstrained conversation or reports about other people, typically involving details that are not confirmed as being true; a person who often talks about the details of other people's lives.*

Triangulation: *the formation of or division into triangles; speaking to a third party about something that should be addressed directly with the other person involved.* A linear and much healthier conversation would be *arranged in or extending along a straight or nearly straight line.* That is, go directly to the horse's mouth—no sidestepping to spread the manure around.

Criticism: *to express disapproval of someone or something; to talk about the problems or faults of someone or something.*

> **Note:** I use the word criticism in Safe Souls rather than judgment, but I believe personal judgment is the precursor to criticism, so it should also be avoided. There cannot be one without the other. Judgment is how we assess a person or situation and criticism is an active process that we do to ourselves or others (even if the critical thoughts are left unspoken.) If you nip it in the bud at the judgment stage, it will never blossom into full-blown outward criticism.

No gossip + no triangulation + no criticism = a formula we can effortlessly recall, easily adopt, and readily teach to others. Some of the things my husband used to *say*, he would never even *think* anymore. He said, "My whole way of being has changed." Old dogs absolutely *can* learn new tricks. I'm not implying that my husband is old, or a dog, but you see the point.

The other day we were out for breakfast at The Henry, a local hot spot in Phoenix, and ran into a beautiful, gentile couple whom we had not seen in a number of months. Prior to that, we had often witnessed them enjoying the same Sunday morning ritual—eating their breakfasts and reading their books. While they rarely conversed during these outings, they clearly enjoyed each other and loved their morning routine.

I remembered about eight years ago, when I first met this couple in a different coffee shop, Ken had said, "They never even talk to each other. They literally just sit there and read. Weird. It's probably a bad marriage."

I mentioned his comment from years earlier about that same couple, "Do you remember when you used to criticize their morning interaction, or lack thereof?"

He said, "I know, I can't even believe that was my way of thinking."

That's the Safe Souls formula working—it changes the way you interact with your world. Be it the inner world of your thoughts or the outer world of your words and actions.

1% MILK STORY

Chip Heath and Dan Heath wrote a book called, *Switch: How to Change Things When Change is Hard*, and it highlights why simply saying, "Be kind," is not effective. We have to be more specific. According to the Heaths, sometimes resistance to change is not really resistance at all, but rather an authentic lack of clarity.

Two researchers, Steve Booth-Butterfield and Bill Reger, professors at West Virginia University, conducted an interesting experiment. They wanted to figure out a way for people in a certain region to lose weight. They understood that just telling people to eat healthily would not be effective because it lacked specificity. This can happen when a doctor gives a patient vague instructions such as, "You're overweight and you have to lower your cholesterol." It may be a true statement, but the immediate question is, "How?"

In the experiment, Reger and Butterfield decided that the best way to tackle the weight loss issue was to encourage one specific change: have people switch from whole milk to 1% or skim milk. One glass of whole milk has the same amount of saturated fat as 5 strips of bacon, so just this one change could help significantly in overall weight reduction.

The duo suspected that even just *telling* people to drink low fat milk would not be effective, so they needed to make sure people actually had 1% or skim milk at home. They knew consumers usually use what is readily available. So Reger and Butterfield created an advertising campaign that encouraged people to *buy* low fat milk, rather than its full-fat counterpart, as a strategy for healthier living.

They now had a *clear* and *specific* formula for their advertising campaign. They aired the commercials on television for two weeks and, at a press conference, they even displayed a tube of fat to show how much was contained in a gallon of whole milk. The message was clear: to lose weight and decrease your cholesterol levels, start buying 1% or skim milk. If it was the only option in the fridge, that's what people would drink. It's that simple.

The results were impressive. Rider and Butterfield monitored milk sales in eight stores in the region where the commercials were airing. Before the advertisement aired, only 18 percent of the milk sales were skim or 1% milk. During the campaign, that number rose to 41 percent. The researchers went back six months later and the numbers were holding at 35 percent.

The point is that if we want macro-level changes, we need micro-level specifics. Just saying, "Be kind to one another," is too vague. People might agree this is a great idea, but without any direction or specifics on *how* to be more kind, change would be unlikely. The other problem is that people have different definitions of kindness. In the development of Safe Souls, I spent time analyzing the most basic ways we can be kind to one another. The three concepts—no gossip, no triangulation, and no criticism—created the perfect framework upon which people can act. The clearer the direction, the more significant the change, the safer the soul. In addition to No GTC, the four Tools for Transformation are definitive ways to increase your kindness quotient, as are the Fourth and Fifth Dimensions. I will expand on these concepts later.

SAFE SOULS AS A SPIRITUAL PRACTICE

Safe Souls is more than just a formula for creating a better workplace, a more loving family, or a more cohesive group of friends, Safe Souls offers a spiritual lesson. Love and kindness—which permeate most every religion and spiritual practice—is its basis. It presents a foundation for respect, community, and ultimately, peace among its practitioners. The principles are so simple yet they have a profound impact upon everyone they touch...and they are not new.

What has been will be again, what has been done will be
done again; there is nothing new under the sun.

~ Ecclesiastes 1:9

When Safe Souls was percolating, I realized I was tapping into a truth that has been taught globally for millennia through most major religions, philosophical ideologies, and spiritual disciplines. While the concepts prescribed in Safe Souls are not new, they are stripped of all religious dogma so their application can be simple and universal. In Chapter 8 however, we will explore some of the ancient religions and philosophies, as well as some current ideologies, that are aligned with the precepts of Safe Souls.

CHAPTER 2

SAFE SOULS KEY #1: NO GOSSIP

A life filled with silly social drama and gossip indicates that a person is disconnected from purpose and lacking meaningful goals. People on a path of purpose don't have time for drama.

~ Brendon Burchard, Best Selling Author of *The Charge*

GOSSIP

I agree with psychologists, thought leaders, and theorists, who believe that people engage in gossip because of its social pull. It can cause people to feel a sense of connection. It can give people perceived validation if the listener agrees with them. It can make people feel better, often at the expense of others. Interestingly though, it has been said that gossipers ultimately feel powerless, unworthy, insecure, afraid, jealous, or fearful, and use other people to try to buoy themselves up. According to the *European Journal of Social Psychology*,[1] individuals who are perceived to engage in gossiping regularly are seen as having less social power and as being less liked. Ultimately, gossiping is not successful in creating that desired for and true connection, as the gossiper becomes less powerful and less trustworthy in the wake of his words.

This dissipation of power and positivity leaves him feeling bad, disconnected, and not trusted. It even changes him energetically.

---

1. Farley, S. "Is gossip power? The inverse relationship between gossip, power, and likability." *European Journal of Social Psychology* (2011): 41, 574-579.

When we emit negativity, this is what we will receive back. There are studies that show our actual cells changing size, shape, and activity depending on the words we speak or the emotions we entertain. Cellular biologist Bruce Lipton, Ph.D., author of *The Biology of Belief*, and *Spontaneous Evolution*, states, "Each cell membrane has receptors that pick up various environmental signals and this mechanism controls the 'reading' of the genes inside your cells. Your cells can choose to read or not read the genetic blueprint depending on the signals being received from the environment. So having a 'cancer program' in your DNA does not automatically mean you're destined to get cancer. Far from it. This genetic information does not ever have to be expressed."

He states that there are genetic controls in your cells that can either be switched on or off depending on the environment. He believes that our genes can even be changed by our mood or emotions.

Konstantin Eriksen also supports this in his article, *The Science of Epigenetics: How Our Minds Can Reprogram Our Genes*,[2] and refers to an experiment done in 1988 by British molecular biologist, John Cairns.

Eriksen writes, "Cairns took bacteria whose genes did not allow them to produce lactase, the enzyme needed to digest milk sugar, and placed them in petri dishes where the only food present was lactose. Much to his astonishment, within a few days, all of the petri dishes had been colonized by the bacteria and they were eating lactose. The bacterial DNA had changed in response to its environment. This experiment has been replicated many times and they have not found a better explanation than this obvious fact—even primitive organisms can evolve consciously.

"So, information flows in both directions, from DNA to proteins and from proteins to DNA, contradicting the 'central dogma' that information flow is a one-way street. Genes can be activated and deactivated by signals from the environment. The consciousness of the cell is inside the cell's membrane. Each and every cell

---

2. Eriksen, K. (http://wakeup-world.com/2012/03/26/the-science-of-epigenetics-how-our-minds-can-reprogram-our-genes/)

in our bodies has a type of consciousness. Genes change their expression depending on what is happening outside our cells and even outside our bodies."

Eriksen concluded that, "Our beliefs can change our biology. We have the power to heal ourselves, increase our feelings of self-worth and improve our emotional state. Every aspect of our lives can be improved with the right intention.

"The worst thing we can do, as thinking and feeling people, is to get cut off from our deep, positive emotions and let fear and anger take over our lives. When we allow ourselves to be taken over by negativity, we are putting ourselves in a mental-biological state of fear akin to the fight-or-flight response.

"In order to grow positively as human beings, we need to express positive emotions such as love, affection, joy and a will to conquer ourselves and our own lives. When we change our beliefs, we change our emotional states. When that happens, we change our lives."

This is not just the power of positive thinking or the law-of-attraction mumbo jumbo—this is science. Most of us do not understand the power of our thoughts and our words. If we did, we would regulate them much more wisely.

GOSSIP AND PERCEIVED SAFETY

Gossip also seems to fuel our innate, DNA-sponsored desire, and I might even go as far as to say our *need,* to fit in. This is a foundational issue stemming from our cavemen ancestors' need for a communal sense of safety. Once tribes grew too large to be close-knit, people would create 'tribes within the tribes' by gossiping. The theory was that if you were 'against' them, you were 'with' us—you were safe. This behavior might have been necessary for survival in the Stone Age, but in modernity, negative gossip ultimately reduces our power and confidence. If we understood that low self-esteem and a desire to 'fit in' are frequently cited as motivations for workplace gossip, we may not engage in it as readily. Especially if our colleagues are also aware that gossip might be an indicator of these less-than-noble character traits.

This begs the question, "Why do we really do it?" According to DiFonzo and Bordia, authors of *Rumor Psychology: Social and Organizational Approaches*,[3] there are five essential functions that gossip has in the workplace:

1. It helps individuals learn social information about other individuals in the organization (often without even having to meet the other individual).

2. It builds social networks of individuals by bonding co-workers together and affiliating people with each other.

3. It breaks existing bonds by ostracizing individuals within an organization.

4. It enhances one's social status/power/prestige within the organization.

5. It informs individuals as to what is considered socially acceptable behavior within the organization.

Some of this may sound helpful and positive, but the negative consequences of workplace gossip may also include:

• Lost productivity and wasted time

• Erosion of trust and morale

• Increased anxiety among employees as rumors circulate without any clear information as to what is fact and what is fiction

• Growing divisiveness among employees as people 'take sides'

• Hurt feelings and reputations

• Jeopardized chances for the gossipers' advancement, as

3. Nicholas DiFonzo, PhD and Prashant Bordia, PhD. *Rumor Psychology: Social and Organizational Approaches* Copyright: 2007. American Psychological Association (APA).

they are perceived as unprofessional

- Attrition as good employees leave the company due to the unhealthy work atmosphere

In my view, the negatives far outweigh the positives. And praising people rather than dissing them can accomplish all the positive consequences listed above without the hidden and costly effect of decreased productivity. Smiljan Mori, CEO of Smiljan Mori Success Systems and The MindOver™ Network says, "Gossip is the single biggest way to ensure a decrease in productivity within an organization." Why wouldn't we simply choose the kind, clean, and clear communication channel?

I also believe that gossip is a form of bullying. Bullying can be defined as: *the activity of repeated, aggressive behavior intended to hurt another person, physically or mentally. Bullying is characterized by an individual behaving in a certain way to gain power over another person.*

Norwegian researcher Dan Olweus says bullying occurs when a person is, "exposed, repeatedly and over time, to negative actions on the part of one or more other persons." He says negative actions occur, "when a person intentionally inflicts injury or discomfort upon another person, through physical contact, through words or in other ways."

This is why gossip is so damaging and why it causes people's souls to feel so unsafe. Even if they never hear the spoken words, they are picking up on the negative energy in the room and in their relationships.

As a caveat, of course I can't say I have never gossiped. It seems to be a human default. But as soon as I've engaged in gossip, I recognize it and feel ashamed. Then I do my best to right any wrongs I have committed by gossiping. I use the SOAP method. It brings healing and freedom for both the listener and user. It also releases the subject of the gossip from any negative energy. I will describe this technique later in this chapter.

Having been on the receiving end of much bullying and gossip, perhaps I'm extra sensitive to it, but I'm grateful for my trials, as they caused creation. I had to experience the darkness in order to embrace the light. I had to feel unsafe in order to create Safe Souls.

LORD OF THE FLIES

A number of years ago, a few friends and I put together a motorcycle charity ride. I will keep the name of the tour and the people involved private, to avoid falling into the realm of gossip. This is simply to delve deeper into the Safe Souls distinction.

We set out on our motorbikes to ride through all 48 contiguous states and the 10 Canadian provinces, raising half a million dollars through our efforts. During the two-month endurance tour, we shared the important message of cancer *prevention* via live radio and TV shows, scheduled speaking events, print media, and simply talking with people while stopping at about 200 different gas stations to fill up our tanks and at as many restaurants as we paused for meals.

Our mission was:

To raise awareness for cancer prevention by:
   1. educating on ways to adopt a truly healthy lifestyle,
   2. educating on how to reduce or eliminate cancer-causing
      exposures, and
   3. educating on natural options for cancer prevention and
      treatment.

We worked for two years planning, securing sponsorships, creating the route, filing for our charitable status, preparing promotional items, and were in the process of making a documentary. To say I was excited to positively impact many lives would be a gross understatement.

On the first day out, in fact, at our first stop—the Canadian/ U.S. border crossing line-up just south of our hometown of Vancouver—my primary partner on the project, who had vowed to not light up visibly during the tour, and another team member, pulled out a cigarette and a cigarillo respectively and proceeded to smoke. There we were, wearing our cancer prevention logoed leather jackets behind our 70-foot rig promoting cancer prevention (a 40-foot chase RV with a 30-foot trailer loaded up with extra motorbikes, presentation material, etc.), and my teammates were flashing their cancer sticks.

I was shocked. "What the heck? This is not really happening!" (I'm sure my language was much stronger in the moment.) Needless to say, a fairly heated private conversation ensued and they promised to refrain from smoking while in public. But the incident already started a downward spiral and, as the tour progressed, problems went from bad to worse. My primary partner had been totally sober for the ten months leading up to the tour, but as soon as we hit the road, he and his smoking partner hit the bottle. Being the life of the party quickly became more important than our mission—actually saving lives.

I said, "We've known each other a long time and our usual rides are all about the fun and adventure, but this is different. We are promoting cancer prevention and you're smoking publically and getting drunk every night? What!? Let's fast-forward… how would our sponsors, or anyone for that matter, react to a photo in the media or on our tour's Facebook page showing you guys smoking and doing shots?" We had a number of $50,000 sponsorships from wealthy individuals and companies and we had many $20 donations from people who could hardly afford rent. We accepted this support as I thought we were all committed to our cause. I could not help thinking about how our backers would react to seeing this. It would be a slap in their faces. I thought of our supporters as shareholders and felt we had a serious responsibility to them.

Early on, I discovered the team was even using our petty cash for a beer and cocktail fund. When I questioned this in the daily post-ride meeting, I was made to feel like a killjoy. They cited it was being allocated to the 'Hospitality' line item on our expense report. Really? I've served on various non-profit boards for over 20 years and I've never seen the hospitality budget blown on booze for the board of directors. They eventually saw their error and announced they had created an alcohol slush fund, but by then I had already been rejected for my integrity—or perhaps for pointing out their lack of such. Later on I also learned that one of the girls was using donations to fly home for a break. What!? When I questioned the integrity of the decision, she simply said, "Lori, I thought you were my friend." I guess we just have very different views on fiscal responsibility. I saw the generous faces of the countless people who had donated, even out of their scarcity, and felt very responsible to them. This was not a popular stance.

It's ironic because my friends and family were so concerned about my physical safety on the road, but little did they know that the biggest wounds I would receive were from my fellow teammates. Even as I write this, I have a sense that readers might think I was being a stuffed shirt, but I am anything but that. I love a good shimmy-shake and adore throwing caution to the wind on an adventure. I simply took our responsibly seriously and couldn't accept that they were modeling such blatant cancer causing activities and that our donor's money was being used fraudulently. Who knew my stand for integrity would ultimately get me thrown off the proverbial island?

I was totally hamstrung. Through a majority vote, they even refused Ken's offer of free labor for a summer intern, who had a heart for cancer prevention, to phone ahead and set up nightly events. This would have helped us fulfill on our mission—a task that our hired event coordinator was supposed to be doing, but wasn't. But my partners refused the help—it would mean they actually had to work rather than just party each night. I could go on with similar stories, but I'll conclude by saying that on day 55 of the 65-day event, I finally pulled our sponsorship—my husband and I had funded the motorhome, gas, driver, and all related expenses—and ended my involvement in the tour. I said, "I can't, in good faith, roll back into Vancouver as if everything is okay. And we are not spending any more valuable resources on you guys." It really became clear that for them it was a joy ride, not a mission, and I was out. My suspicion as to where their hearts laid was confirmed when they sabotaged the motorhome after removing their belongings. Yes, two grown men vandalized about $10,000 worth of promotional decals wrapping our rig.

Ken came to me after the dust had settled and said, "I watched that whole thing go down. It was the *Lord of the Flies* on motorbikes. I'm surprised you stuck with it as long as you did."

Leaving the tour was not an easy decision, but when my stand for what was right and honorable continually had me excluded from the group, I had to protect myself. My soul was just not safe. I am not sharing this for sympathy, but, for me, this was a case of a few grown adults who just couldn't handle being called out on their dishonorable behavior. Instead of acknowledging it and moving on, they decided to shoot the messenger. One even said somewhere near Charleston, West Virginia, "I don't want to ride with you anymore." Even though I made the decision to physically leave and pull our sponsorship, the team had already rejected me. The next day, I boarded a plane—heartbroken, but feeling so full of integrity—and headed home. I was two states and three Canadian provinces short of the goal, but I was no longer going to sponsor the unsafe souls and put myself in harm's way.

The point of this story is simply to highlight that in some organizations there are going to be bad apples. Not everyone will be on board with what you are trying to accomplish and may even try to sabotage your efforts. I heard an acronym recently—HATERS: Having Anger Toward Everyone Reaching Success—and these people are out there. When you come across one of these individuals, the best ways to handle them is with kindness—kindly escort them to the door. In the above case, I waited way too long to do so, but I was resistant to the lesson I was being challenged to learn. I should have taken a stand as soon as I felt unsafe. The writing was on the wall; I was just unwilling to read it. I literally *felt* the gossip and murmuring behind my back, which came out in spades after the tour, but I couldn't face it in the moment. Perhaps I was too afraid of rejection, so I continued to give grace and have hope. But their gossip was literally a social cancer amid us—and it polarized the whole team. Quite ironic given that our mission was to eliminate the avoidable causes of cancer. *Gossip is social cancer.* It harms, and even kills, people. But some are totally resistant to the No GTC formula. If people cannot embrace Safe Souls, having a healthy and hasty willingness to let them go will serve you well.

HOW DO WE STOP THE CYCLE?

If you grew up with a Safe Soul mom like I did, you often heard, "If you don't have anything nice to say then don't say anything at all." It is a great reminder and a habit former. It really can be this simple. Just stop doing it. The popular acronym THINK holds so true. Before you speak, **THINK** !

Is what you are about to say:

- True?
- Helpful?
- Inspiring?
- Necessary?
- Kind?

The Golden Rule is also worth adhering to: *Do unto others as you would have them do unto you.* Another effective litmus test is to ask yourself, "Would I like to be the topic of conversation I am hearing or having right now?" If not, then zip it.

Talking 'behind someone's back' in a *kind* way—what I call 'positive gossip'—is always appropriate though! I love doing this. And I also love it when others do the same. When I hear positive gossip, I always make a point of either calling the topic of the gossip or writing him or her a quick email saying, "Hey, I just wanted you to know that John was talking about you behind your back today and he thinks you're a total rock star!" I get detailed about what was said—specifics are always more powerful than generalities. This makes me smile as I write or share and I'm sure it makes the recipient of the praise even happier. It is a perfect way to cultivate Safe Souls. When someone knows they are being praised, it is one of the surest paths to their feeling loved, appreciated, and well, safe.

If you are in the company of critics and gossips and you are taking a stand against it, you may feel like a lone voice, like the killjoy, like an odd ball. But I encourage you to share the Safe Souls distinction and to remind people that the listener is as guilty of gossiping as the speaker. You can be the light. For some people, gossip is so habitual, that, even if they are not intentionally malicious, their behavior is. They are simply in the dark and need you to bring them into the light. Encourage them to stop gossiping. Ask them to consider how the subject of the gossip would feel if they were a fly on the wall. You can also share the effects of gossip on the gossiper—the false sense of connection that ultimately leaves them feeling alone. If presented in a non-judgmental and non-confrontational way, this message is usually met with grace. If it's not, these might not be the friends for you.

This brings up the question of judgment. Some might ask, "Am I not judging someone as being a gossip or being critical? Am I not guilty of GTC also?" As long as you are not forming an unfair opinion about someone and criticizing him or her, then I think you are still in the Safe Soul Zone. Humans are, in fact, always making judgments...will I make it across the street without getting hit? Will that person be a good life partner? Is he the best marketer for our company? Judging is necessary for survival and evolution. It's what we do with our judgment that can be the issue. Be careful with it. Don't use it to form a negative opinion about someone, something, or some situation.

If you have shared your views about the effects of gossiping and the person is constitutionally incapable of ceasing, you would be doing yourself a favor by leaving his presence. Not only is he bringing you down in the moment, we also take on character traits of those we spend the most time with long-term. And who wants to become a gossip? In addition, if he is gossiping about others, guess what's happening when *you* leave the room? Hang around people you aspire to be like.

SOME JUST *HAVE* TO GTC!

I had an experience where it became necessary to 'break up' with a new girlfriend. We were introduced by a mutual friend and had only been for coffee a few times when she suddenly began speaking negatively about our friend. I would stop her and defend the person, but I think it fell on deaf ears. I felt really uncomfortable and conflicted. She was otherwise a lovely person, but my trust for her was ebbing. The next time she asked me to get together, I said that I would, but only if our friend's name never came into the conversation. If she could honor that, I'd love to spend time with her. If not, then I couldn't. She agreed that his name would not come up, but when we met, she did not honor her word. I had to cut her off mid-sentence and insist she stopped sharing an issue that was none of my (or her) business. When she wouldn't, I had to leave the conversation. She was just too hell-bent on gossiping. We have not been out since.

This may sound quite harsh, but the Safe Soul stand is so simple for people who don't gossip, triangulate, or criticize. It's even easy for those who still do, but are committed to breaking the habit. Many even welcome the accountability. These are the people with whom I choose to spend time. Others, I can love from afar, but they cannot be part of my circle of close confidants.

WASH YOUR MOUTH OUT WITH SOAP

If you suddenly find yourself engaged in gossip (the human condition can have us sucked in quite quickly and easily), wash your mouth out with proverbial **SOAP**.

- **S**top
- **O**wn it
- **A**pologize
- **P**raise

It's great leadership—and friendship—to interject a negative conversation with a..."Whoa! How did we get here? (**S**top.) We are in full-blown gossip. (**O**wn it.) I deeply apologize for my part in it as this is not who I'm committed to being. (**A**pologize.) And this is not fair to Susan. She is an incredible mother, worker, friend, etc. (**P**raise.)" Try to find as many things to *praise* her for as you have just lambasted her for, or more. This praise is *positive gossip* and it's a generous practice.

If a conversation has been derailed by gossip, triangulation, or criticism, the SOAP method is an easy way to get it back on track. Everyone will feel better for it. Especially Susan, and she was not even in the room. (If we think that the subject of our gossip isn't aware of it, we are surely mistaken. Intuition is an incredibly powerful survival instinct.)

If we can't seem to stop gossiping for another's sake, once we really understand that 'what comes around truly does go around,' then we have an incentive to quit. We will be treated as we treat others. It's that simple.

WHAT ABOUT MANAGING TEAMS?

There are really only a few situations that call for 'talking behind someone's back.' One of them is when you are managing people. Another is if a person's safety is at risk, such as during a drug intervention. Another is in a professional and confidential relationship, as with a paid counselor, who is helping you work through an interpersonal issue. Lastly, there is also a place for discussing people or situations in what we call a 'Committed Conversation for Action.' In each case, if everyone converses in a kind and healthy way, has the intention of improving a situation,

ε person's soul intact, the subject will ultimately
honored. The Committed Conversation for Action
ools of Transformation, and is expounded on later

...aging people and teams while avoiding gossip can be tricky—discussing subordinates, team members, processes, and systems are part of a manager's responsibility. So is judging performance. We need to continually assess people in order to run a healthy business. I've witnessed gracious and safe leaders and I've witnessed malicious and unsafe ones. But managing teams and being a Safe Soul do not have to be mutually exclusive. If we lead with the intention of leaving everyone's soul intact and the business thriving, we will have been successful in operating as a Safe Soul.

I was part of a board of directors running a non-profit event and one of the staff members was unable to accomplish his work due to some circumstantial restrictions. The board agreed that his frustration was bringing the team's energy down and his lack of efficacy was not supporting his costly salary and travel expenses. We discussed the issue, everyone agreed another solution was necessary, and each board member offered a variety of ideas. In the end, we decided he and the business would be better off by executing his responsibilities within a different set of parameters. As an executive board, we did have to discuss the situation 'behind his back' for the sake of the mission and to be responsible to our budget and other commitments. We discussed the issues with the intention of empowering him and keeping his soul safe. It was a Committed Conversation for Action. A caveat here: everyone on the team needs to honor the facts of the discussion or such conversations can be misinterpreted, misconstrued, misquoted, and ultimately very damaging.

THE GOSSIPING CHEFS

One crisp sunny afternoon, I was enjoying lunch on the patio of a quaint little vegan cafe in Phoenix. It's known for being all Zen and yogic and peaceful and full of, well, love. I smiled when I overheard the head chef chatting with a young gal who had obviously just started working there. I couldn't help overhearing their lovely conversation. The chef was praising her young protégé. "Your work is amazing. You have been such a welcome addition to the team in the last few weeks. You clearly have a fantastic work ethic and we would like to promote you to a full time position." The conversation went on like that for a while. There were many praises back and forth and I thought, "What a couple of sweet, focused, and passionate humans." Their interaction wanted me to eat there more often—it just felt good.

Until things crumbled.

The manager said, "We are relieved to be seeing less of Nick. I can't tell you how many times we've told him to shape up and perform better. I mean, just the other day, he made a judgment call as to whether or not to receive an order of mint from the supplier's delivery. He thought we had ordered too much so he only accepted half the shipment. Can you believe it? I mean, we ended up running out and I had to get some at Trader Joe's. It's *my* call as to what we should receive or not!" (Note that the grocery store was less than 100 feet from the restaurant.)

The trainee went on to say, "I know, the other day he did . . . blah, blah, blah." Ten minutes later, they were still talking about how bad this guy was. Partway through, the head honcho went on to say how dumb Nick was for accepting a large lettuce order the other day as they wound up having to waste some heads. Huh? Was he supposed to make decisions or not? She was sending so many mixed messages to this new hire. One of which was, "Don't ever risk making a decision because if you do, and you screw up, I will be broadcasting it behind your back to the rest of the team!" Not a very empowering message, even if delivered completely unconsciously.

The details of the conversation aren't even really what piqued my interest. (Though it was a good example of how witnessing malicious gossip can be a wet blanket.) The germane piece was the interesting dynamic that occurred. As soon as they started gossiping about their colleague, their body language mutated. They sat up and leaned forward. They connected on a different level. They became animated. They started speaking faster. It was fascinating. I believe this is what gossip does—it creates a false sense of connection.

As a customer witnessing this, I felt slimed. It made me want to avoid that restaurant altogether. This was not the loving vegan juju I had grown to adore from this café—the energy had become unbearably negative. In fact, as I sit and write this chapter, I realize that I have never been back to that café. And I used to love it.

There is obviously a place for constructive and committed critique in the workplace. This is the purpose of structured and specific daily, weekly, quarterly, or annual reviews. And of course, as managers and leaders, we need the freedom to discuss people under our tutelage, but it should be done privately with other leaders and for the purpose of developing the person and advancing the business. The kind of backbiting gossip I had just witnessed does neither.

Exercise #1: Gossip, Triangulation, and Criticism vs. Productivity, Creativity, and Happiness

Write down a time or situation when you sensed you were being gossiped about, you were the subject of triangulation, or you were being outwardly and unkindly criticized. How did this affect your productivity, creativity, and overall happiness at work, at school, or with your friends and family members? How did you feel?

_____

_____

_____

_____

_____

_____

_____

Now write down a time where you felt you were part of the team, where you felt safe and appreciated, and where you knew everyone had your back. How did this affect your productivity, creativity, and overall happiness? How did you feel?

_____

_____

_____

_____

_____

_____

Compare and ask yourself...where do productivity, creativity, and happiness go within each example? How can you be the change you'd like to see in each environment?

_____

_____

_____

_____

_____

_____

_____

_____

CHAPTER 3

SAFE SOULS KEY #2: NO TRIANGULATION

The single biggest problem in communication
is the illusion that it has taken place.
~ George Bernard Shaw

As stated in Chapter 1, triangulation occurs when one person has an issue with another person, but instead of going directly to that person, he vents to a third party. No real communication occurs between the two primary parties, but rather a *triangle* of communication is created with someone totally separate from the pertinent issue.

The following story is a perfect example of how troublesome triangulation can be.

RECYCLING IN SUMMERLAND

A few years ago, I went from hero to zero by one bin of garbage and a side of triangulation.

Here's what happened.

Ken and I have a lake home in Canada and his amazing parents live right next door. We cherish them and love visiting throughout the summer. Omi and Opi are not the proverbial problematic parents-in-laws; they are my buddies and I love them to bits. Time spent together is full of love, giggles, dog walks, card games, happy hours, and their cooking...oh, their cooking!

Suffice to say, we have massive love and respect for one another.

One rainy Saturday morning, I busied myself by cleaning out a storage closet filled with years worth of old junk. There were tapes, CDs, tchotchkes, outdated yellow pages, home movies, broken tennis racquets, badminton equipment, volleyballs, board games, outdoor sports equipment, etc. You get the picture. It was the put-everything-here-that-you-don't-know-what-to-do-with spot. I emptied all the contents into the hallway and proceeded to piece-by-piece organize, store, fix, or chuck what I had found. I created a pile of items I suspected we wanted to toss but, since none of those items were mine, I needed to ask Ken first. When he saw the pile of long forgotten items, he said to just throw them away. So I did. I decided to further Feng Shui the place and used the reclaimed closet shelving for the sports equipment and outdoor patio pillows that had been dumped in a spare room. I was pleased with the results and everyone else thought it was a job well done. The rest of the weekend was full of laughter, fun, and good connecting. It was light and easy.

The next time we went up to the lake, however, there was a totally different energy. I'm sure you have felt the type of shift I am referring to. You walk into a room and suddenly your intuition says, "Beware!" You know something is wrong, but you can't quite put your finger on it. The fight-or-flight survival instinct, which has been in our genes since we were cavemen, kicks in immediately. This instinct tells us that something is ready to pounce on us and we either need to be ready to run or to fight. It is our early warning system.

These days, we don't have to worry about tigers jumping out of the bush, but our innate survival instincts are still part of our DNA. Sometimes we can just tell if someone is talking about us or means us harm. There is nothing too mystical about it when you consider how much information your brain processes every waking second. Your unconscious mind is a passive observer and can notice clues in the environment that your conscious mind sometimes misses. In this case, it was my normally chipper, loving, and inclusive father-in-law's obvious heaviness and distancing.

I was getting the cold shoulder from Opi and even from my always-sweet mother-in-law. This was evidence of classic triangulation. I spoke to Ken about it and he said it was all in my head. I was being overly sensitive; there was nothing the matter. But I knew there was something wrong and I've learned to trust my 'Spidey' sense. The silence from Opi was deafening and his lack of warmth was completely out of character. I did not feel safe whatsoever.

I put off acting on my intuition for an uncomfortable day or so, but I finally plucked up the courage to go next door to speak with Opi. We needed a 'Clearing Conversation.' (See pp.91,92.)

He was sitting on the patio in the shade reading The Globe and Mail. When I approached him, he just barely lowered it enough for me to see his eyes. It was a literal barrier. I asked him if we could talk. He slowly lowered the paper and I sat down somewhat reluctantly on the ottoman.

"Is there anything bothering you, Opi?" I asked.

"No, nothing at all," he said.

But I knew better. I'd felt the chill in the air. So I pressed. "Opi, I know there's something bothering you. Can we please talk about it? Have I done something to upset you?"

"No, all is good."

"Really? Opi, you and Omi have been super distant towards me this weekend and I can tell 100% that there is something on your mind. I hope we have a deep enough friendship that we can come to each other when we need to. There's nothing you could say that would hurt me more than a passive-aggressive approach like the silent treatment. Please, tell me what's on your mind."

"Well, ok then. I feel like a Joe-boy around here! Who do you think was going to separate all the garbage from the closet items you threw out? Don't you know there are strict recycling rules here?"

Bingo! He had probably spent parts of the last few weeks stewing on this and the entire time I was in his presence trying not to blow his lid. All this pent-up emotion was weighing heavily on him. I could see it. His shoulders were hunched over and he was not smiling, laughing, nor engaging.

When he 'fessed up, I felt like a total *shmoe*. Of course, I should have recycled the phone book and a few of the other items! For sure it was a complete error in judgment. I grew up in Vancouver where recycling was part of our normal household activities. But after living in Phoenix for a few years—where separating the recycling from the garbage happens mainly at the dump—I had gotten out of the habit of meticulously dividing household trash. At the lake, I'd simply had a mind burp. I would never think something like, "I'll just throw it in here; Opi will separate it." No way!

This was a classic example of triangulation. Instead of coming to me—the source of his complaint—he had gone to Omi and vented his frustration. It's not that Opi is a bad person for doing this; it's just the default way that most humans operate. I know he loves me and never intentionally meant to hurt me, but triangulation *is* very hurtful. And when Omi listened to his complaints, they inadvertently created 'agreement reality.' This is when two or more people agree on something (whether it's true or not) and since they agree on it, it becomes factual to them. In this case, the agreement reality might have been: "Lori is BAD! Who would ever do such a thing and just expect us to rummage through the garbage to pick out the recycling items. Yes, she is a bad person. Let's give her the cold shoulder next time she comes to the lake."

Of course this is not exactly how I think the conversation went, but the outcome was the same. Omi somewhat adopted Opi's frustration and I was the receiver of the tainted energy. Their usual loving warmth and openness became cool reservation. And because it created an aggressive environment, albeit a passive one,

I did not feel safe. Trust had been broken, communication had failed, and I felt like my in-laws perception of me was wrong and unfair. Could they really believe I had so little regard for them? I had to change the environment back to one of love and trust.

Once Opi was able to share what was real for him, I was able to nurture his heart by telling him how much I love him and how thankful Ken and I are for everything he does to keep the properties running so smoothly. I was able to say that I would never do something so disrespectful towards him because I respect him so much! Then I asked him to make a deal with me. If we EVER had something between us, we would trust each other enough to come and share it directly. There were tears, hugs, and the energy was clean again.

Next was Omi.

I sat with her and shared what had just occurred with Opi and I told her I was very sorry for the recycling mistake. I explained that it was an error in action, not an error in attitude. I confirmed my love and respect for them and said that I would never do anything purposely to harm them. Again, there were tears, hugs, and the energy was renewed.

While this was, in the end, a beautiful time of connection, it was a painful way to get there. Had Safe Souls been in operation to begin with, Opi would have simply called me up on garbage day and said something like, "Hey, did you know that there are strict recycling rules here? I had to spend twenty minutes rummaging through the garbage! Next time, please make sure that recyclables go in the blue box. And if you're unsure about what goes where, there is a list posted above the garbage can."

"Whoops! Oh my gosh, Opi. I'm so, so sorry. Of course I should have done that. I was so in the groove of cleaning out the closet, and I've gotten into the Phoenix habit of not recycling as diligently, that it did not even occur to me. I'm really sorry. Thanks for letting me know. I'll make sure to separate it in the future. How can I make it up to you?"

(If we were still up at the lake on garbage day, he might have just hauled my butt out to the bin and said, "Please separate this!")

In either case, triangulation would have been non-existent. Straight-line communication and mutual respect would have ensued. Souls would have felt safe. Next time!

KEN IN LAS VEGAS

Avoiding triangulation is also an effective problem solving strategy. If grievances are aired to people who aren't even involved in the issue, then they are not invested in finding a solution. On the other hand, if the problem is addressed directly with the person involved, creative problem solving is possible.

A few years ago, Ken and I went through a period where we were just not spending much time together. Thankfully we are both very independent, but for a short season, I felt our marriage was suffering. I loath bringing a need or disappointment to Ken—I don't want him to feel he's not a good enough husband or I need more of him than he can give. He's an amazing partner, but when I have raised an issue in the past, he has often become very defensive saying, "I'm busy working for us! I'm providing for the family. How can you make me wrong for that?"

I learned to keep quiet.

As time passed and I reflected, I concluded that keeping quiet was not going to solve the problem. I was often tempted to take my grievance to a girlfriend or two. We could commiserate and create agreement reality—it was Ken's fault. He should be more available and further, he should *know* that his jam-packed schedule is a matrimonial time bomb. He should start taking some responsibility for his relationship.

Triangulation would have been much easier than confronting Ken. But, my commitment is to us and to having the best marriage possible, so I plucked up the courage and shared what was missing for me. Time. Undistracted time with my husband.

To my shock, he just listened. He allowed me to 'empty my basket' and was simply present to my words and my feelings. What was going on here? He told me later that his blood pressure was so high he felt like he was going to explode. It was all he could do to hold his tongue. But he did. Actually, he didn't hold his tongue completely. He said, "Yes, I've got it. I hear you." What? This was awesome. I felt so much better for having shared my heart. We went on to have a wonderful evening. I felt super connected to Ken and my love for him deepened even further.

What happened next was the cool part. His willingness to just listen and not defend himself had me want to take the 100% responsible viewpoint. So I asked myself, "What can *I* do that will enable us to spend more time together?" Rather than waiting for Ken to come up with something, I got proactive and devised a plan.

Normally, Ken and I go to bed at the same time. But since I need one more hour of sleep than he does, he always arose one hour earlier and took his exercise. He would just be finishing his program when I got up and dashed off for my workout class or a run. We were apart for one of the activities we love to do together: exercise.

Then in the evenings, when we were not out entertaining clients or socializing with friends, we would get home, have a bite, and Ken would dive into that day's hundred or so emails. I would read, watch a show, or do my chores around the house. We were occupying the same space, but we were not really together. It was not sustainable.

I proposed a plan out of my desire for, and my commitment to, an amazing, fun, loving marriage. I asked Ken, "What if I go to bed one hour earlier than you do and then we get up at the same time to exercise? That way we get an extra five hours of fun together during the week."

He loved it! And the side benefit that I hadn't even thought of was that just him knowing he had one hour while I was in bed at night to get his emails done, freed him up to be present mentally during and after dinner. It was a total win-win. Now, if I had taken the easy and unsafe route and triangulated—taking my complaint to another person—I would not have had Ken's gentle heart as he listened to me. This tenderness made me *want* to come up with a plan. A girlfriend would have likely just sided with me and it would have become a frothy mess.

The lesson: be 100% responsible for your happiness and don't triangulate. This is a recipe for success.

REASONS WE TRIANGULATE

People triangulate if they haven't been taught better communication skills or don't have the courage to talk to the person with whom they really need to talk. But the effect of keeping a grievance or concern from the party involved is unquestionably detrimental. This is why I included the recycling story. I could physically see Opi's whole body, his demeanor, and everything about him being bent over by his internal angst. He had shut down. His face was tense. His joy had evaporated. He was literally suffering, as was I, because he had not approached me with his complaint. He let it fester internally and then shared it with Omi. Once that occurred they both existed in unnecessary turmoil and I could feel it.

Initiating the difficult conversations with both Ken and Opi was my Safe Souls practice. Drawing out Opi's grievance through gentile, probing questions and sharing my concerns with Ken, rather than with someone else, both turned out to be amazing, empowering conversations for us all.

Triangulation is simply about walking in fear. To step out of triangulation and fear you have to step into love and address the appropriate people. It keeps everything much cleaner and leaves no residual ill will in the air. When we use kind, clean, and clear communication we create intimate, rewarding, and healthy relationships. It's the difference between looking out at a crisp, beautiful view when the air is clean and looking out over brown, inhibiting, stifling pollution. A conversation full of integrity and love is crystal clear, while conversing in a cloud of triangulation is a toxic mess.

FORGIVENESS

Forgiveness is also an essential quality for a Safe Soul. Halfway through writing this manuscript, I came across a book called *Safe People—How to Find Relationships That Are Good for You* by Dr. Henry Cloud and Dr. John Townsend. The title *Safe People* had me purchase and read it immediately.

They assert, and I wholeheartedly agree, "Safe relationships are centered and grounded in forgiveness. When you have a friend with the ability to forgive you for hurting her or letting her down, something deeply spiritual occurs in the transaction between you two. You actually experience a glimpse of the deepest nature of God…that's why the forgiving person is safe. The person sees our wrong, yet loves us beyond it. And that love helps heal and transform us into the person God intended us to be. Receiving forgiveness when we know we've truly blown it is a humbling and growth-producing experience. It's the only thing better than forgiving someone else."

Conversely, they write, "Unsafe people are often good at identifying your weaknesses. They can quote the minute and hour you hurt them, and recall the scene in intimate detail and living color. Like a good attorney, they have the entire case mapped out. And you are judged 'guilty.' Yes, we need to be confronted with our weaknesses. Unsafe people, however, confront us not to forgive us, but to condemn and punish us. They remove their love until we are appropriately chastened. This, obviously, destroys any chance for connection or safety."

I love Drs. Cloud and Townsend's teachings on this subject. Forgiveness is exactly what was extended to and from Opi in Summerland and to and from Ken in Las Vegas. Opi forgave me for not recycling and I forgave him for not coming to me directly with his grievance. Ken forgave me for confronting him with my needs and I forgave him for seeming too busy to nurture our marriage.

Exercise #2: Communication and Forgiveness

Have you ever avoided talking through a problem with someone because you haven't felt the freedom to speak your mind? Have you gone to someone else to find support and understanding rather than being direct and speaking right to the person on whom the feelings were focused? How did it turn out? What could you have done differently? Is there someone you need to forgive? Is there someone from whom you need to ask for forgiveness? Write your thoughts below and commit to having Clearing Conversations around what comes up. (See pp.91,92.)

_____

_____

_____

_____

_____

_____

_____

_____

_____

_____

_____

_____

CHAPTER 4

SAFE SOULS KEY #3: NO CRITICISM OR JUDGMENT

Let the refining and improving of your own life keep you
so busy that you have little time to criticize others.

~ H. Jackson Brown, Jr.

CONSTRUCTIVE VS. DESTRUCTIVE CRITICISM

Criticism is a large topic with many nuances. The spectrum runs from concerned and constructive to diminishing and destructive. On one hand, there might be a loving mother who takes her son aside privately to point out that his lifestyle is running amok. Genuine concern for his wellbeing prevails as she shares her perspective. It's a conversation, not an accusation. Yes, she is essentially criticizing his actions, but she does so lovingly, privately, and for his own edification.

On the other hand, there might be a destructive critic who goes around town mouthing off about this same behavior. It is done with no love or grace. He may even criticize privately and directly, which is certainly better than publicly and indirectly, but the spirit behind his words is malicious. He is trying to tear the other down. This is destructive criticism and that which I am speaking about in Safe Souls.

Another thing to understand is that unless we never say another word, never have an opinion, never blaze our own trail, or never accomplish anything publicly, we will be criticized our entire lives. The better we learn to deal with this, the happier we will be. As Aristotle said, "Criticism is something we can avoid easily by saying nothing, doing nothing, and being nothing." Seth Godin also asserts that, "Criticism comes to those who stand out." And I love the late Zig Ziglar's words, "Don't be distracted by criticism. Remember, the only taste of success some people have is when they take a bite out of you."

I wholeheartedly believe that being criticized is a byproduct of a life lived on the court. The sooner we can embrace it, the sooner we will be free from the attachment to needing approval. We will be happier and more liberated. For the sake of Safe Souls, I am asserting that we cannot control what others think or say about us—we will be gossiped about, people will use us as the topic of triangulation, and we will certainly be judged and criticized—but we *can* control what we think or say about others and ourselves. Being on the receiving end of destructive criticism is inevitable; dishing it out is a choice.

This brings us to the nuances of judgment.

> **Judgment:** *the act of forming an opinion or making a decision after careful thought; the act of judging someone or something.*

JUDGMENT VS. PERSONAL JUDGMENT

Judgment is an internal process in which we determine whether something is inherently good or bad. Let's return to our caveman relatives—they had to have a sharp sense of good and bad. This instinct impacted their safety and often their survival. Judgment is an extremely useful tool—a litmus test of sorts—and we use it hundreds of times a day, if not more, without even realizing it as it's often a passive thought process.

Thankfully, for our safety's sake, this judgment instinct is still active today. If a car is travelling too fast for us to make it across the street without being hit, we will wait for it to pass by. If we encounter someone with a knife and he exudes evil energy, we will judge the situation and run. If we are in a position of authority in the workplace, we will assess in order to evaluate someone's occupational performance. Is she hitting the mark in her position? Is his behavior appropriate as a representative of our company? We may also examine character traits within members of a group of associates to see if they are people with whom we want to create close friendships. We may notice a lack of respect among family members and initiate the necessary conversations so the family can operate more smoothly. We may even judge a friend's drug habit and have a loving intervention.

Sounds fine, right? Yes, these are examples of non-malicious judgment. They are either survival tactics or tactics for advancing a business, creating better family dynamics, or causing deeper intimacy among a group of friends. We are always judging and assessing things around us. It's necessary. Especially when we have responsibility for people, a process, or a business. We have to judge and assess constantly for the sake of meeting goals and objectives. What I'm talking about in Safe Souls is when our judgments turn into personal attacks, opinions, and destructive criticisms.

I am referring to maliciously or even passively criticizing a person's appearance, philosophy, political affiliation, religious beliefs, or personal values. It is not about evaluating a person's performance in the workplace or about assessing in order to maintain safety, or even constructively criticizing someone lovingly for their own benefit, it is about criticizing and judging who they are as human beings. The next story demonstrates the effects of personal criticism.

A SLIT FOR A SLUT

Throughout my schooling, our family lived in a fairly affluent neighborhood, but we seemed to be cash poor compared to my classmates. Since we were ten years old, my brother, sister, and I all babysat, had paper routes and, once we were fourteen or fifteen, had our own restaurant or retail jobs. If we wanted more clothes than the annual school allotment of a new pair of runners, a coat, and a few outfits, we had to work for them. (Except for the couple of times my cousin, Corianne, sent me her hand-me-downs. That was like Christmas.) Teaching us to work for the extra things we wanted (all our *needs* were met, just not our *wants*), was one of the most valuable lessons my parents taught us and I'm grateful. Entitlement was definitely not part of our family culture and that has served my brother, sister, and I very well.

With our 9th grade dance fast approaching, most of my girlfriends were happily perusing their stuffed closets planning what cool outfit to wear. I, on the other hand, studied my meager wardrobe and was riddled with anxiety. I had nothing appropriate — rugby pants, a t-shirt, and knock-off North Star runners just weren't going to cut it. I had to go to the mall. My mom didn't enjoy shopping, so clothing and fashion were not really part of my world. I had no idea what to choose, so I went to the one store I had heard was fairly fashionable and not too expensive, Le Chateau. I asked for help from a young, hip-looking sales person — not that I had any clue as to what was hip — as I figured she would know better than I what would be appropriate. I wound up with a dark blue, wool, fairly conservative thigh-length skirt and topped it with a matching blazer and a white long-sleeved, button up tuxedo-style shirt. While the skirt was technically a mini, I looked more like a hostess in a formal restaurant than a young, hip *fashionista*. But I was still proud of my new clothes. They were the first 'fancy' items I had ever purchased.

Those who had more of a fashion sense than I did in those days may have seen right through it — I was just a young girl with no sense of style wearing a bad suit — but when I wore my new outfit to the school dance that weekend, I felt excited, attractive, and feminine for a change — even a little grown up. And the fact that the structured, yet blousy, tuxedo top covered up the dismal reality that I had not...um...blossomed yet, was a major bonus. If I didn't already feel insecure about my lack of clothing—my lack of development was the nail in the coffin of my self-confidence. My brother's friends used to tease me, calling me MB—short for mosquito bites. Hallelujah for blousy tops.

After the dance, we went to a party at the house of one of my best friends. All my girlfriends were there and so was the guy I had had a crush on for a few years. I was so excited—that butterfly-in-the-stomach kind of feeling. And he seemed to be interested in me, too! I had transformed from being a baggy jeans, t-shirt, and running shoe clad girl into a skirt, blouse, and blazer-wearing woman. (At least that's how I felt.) And someone was finally noticing me. Towards the end of the night, my crush and I wound up making out—as it was called back then—and I was over the moon. His kisses were divine and I prayed mine were the same for him. The young innocence of it all—I was sexually inexperienced and naïve. This was a huge deal. I'm sure I was a flurry of hormones, dreams, fears, and every emotion known to a young girl in puppy love.

The next day, I spent a quiet Sunday basking in the memories of it all and curious about what would happen next. Would he invite me out on a date? Would I be his official girlfriend? I had all the thoughts and emotions of a typical teenage girl after her first real kiss with a boy she idolized like a rock star.

This was long before the days of Facebook, Twitter, Instagram, and text messaging. Today, communication around 'the kiss' would have been almost instant. Shoot, I never even used a phone to share the juicy details with my friends. We had one mounted on the wall in the kitchen and one was in my mom's bedroom. Neither was very private, so I simply spent the rest of the weekend savoring the memories, playing my guitar, and keeping what had happened close to my heart.

Maybe it was my soul sensing something was wrong, but I do remember having an uneasy feeling as I walked the few blocks to school on Monday morning. And as I approached my locker, the uneasy feeling rushed from the pit of my stomach, straight to my throat, and choked me. To my absolute horror and utter embarrassment, the word 'SLUT' was written across my locker. My instinct was to lick my finger and rub it off, but it was obviously written with a thick, black, indelible Sharpie pen and was going nowhere. I was so ashamed and humiliated that I just wanted to run and hide and never return. Who wrote this? And who had already seen it!?

Knowing I had to get to class, I quickly opened my locker to retrieve my textbook and then I saw it—an envelope with my name written across the front. Same black Sharpie. I tucked the envelope into my book and ran to class. I didn't learn a thing as I spent the hour reading and re-reading the letter. It was a 9-page diatribe of the ugliest and most hurtful accusations and criticisms. And guess who it was from? My supposed girlfriends. There were five of them and they each took a turn telling me how horrible they thought I was for kissing...we'll call him, John. While I was basking in the memories of the kiss, they had gathered to gossip, triangulate, criticize, and ultimately betray me.

The irony was that some of these girls were already sleeping around, which I certainly was not. I had only kissed a guy and I got publically labeled the slut? And by my best friends?

I later found out that a gal from another school also really liked 'John.' So, because he kissed *me*, I was obviously a man stealer and a slut. I did not just do wrong—I was BAD. The interesting things were that: a) I had no idea someone else liked him, and, b) these were my close girlfriends, so why would they not be happy for me? Most of them didn't even know the 'other' girl very well. Where was the sisterhood?

The written criticisms were lengthy and horrible. One of them said, "Your skirt has a slit fit for a slut. Yup, a slit for a slut." I guess that was the end of my new outfit...and my friendships. I felt alone and ashamed, but also highly confused—while my friends were shaming me, I really didn't believe I had acted shamefully.

I hailed from a very non-communicative family so, at that age, I didn't have the skills, or the audience, to voice my devastation. I could not talk about personal things with my mom, my dad had already moved out, my brother wasn't a safe soul for me back then, my sister had already left for college and, well, my friends had just stabbed me in the back. I did not know how to react so I retreated into myself, sucked it up, and charged on. But ultimately that, and many other similar experiences, had me become fearful in groups of people. My fight-or-flight instincts were always on full alert.

BULLIED FOR BOOZE

I quickly forgave and made up with my friends. Onward marching soldier. However, shortly after that experience, I started drinking quite heavily for a teenager. Looking back, it makes perfect sense—I was numbing painful emotions. My soul was hurting and I needed relief.

Getting booze was easy as, when I was fifteen, I had the perfect fake ID. My sister was the legal drinking age of nineteen so I went into the Department of Motor Vehicles office and pretended to be her. I said I'd lost my wallet and needed a new driver's license. I had practiced her signature to perfection and brought her Social Insurance card, the Canadian version of the U.S. Social Security card, with me for identification. In the early eighties, all they had on file was a person's height, weight, eye color, and hair color. While we were the same coloring, she was taller and a slightly bigger, so I put on high heels and wore a trench coat. After nervously giving my sister's credentials and forging her signature, the administrator took my picture and said, "Thank you, Michelle. Your new license will arrive in the mail within four weeks." I still can't believe the 'balls' I had at fifteen—this was a criminal offense. (And, yes, I thank heavens for the Statute of Limitations and the wisdom I've gained in the last 30 years.)

I soon became a hero among my friends because I had a totally fail-proof, government-issued, fake ID. I was their new, on-demand bootlegger.

For some reason, when I wasn't in the position to do it for them, I didn't have the ability to stand on my own and just say, "No." I didn't even realize saying no was a possibility in those days, but I remember one night I was at my boyfriend's family home, and one of the same group of girls called his house (again, this was long before cell phones) and said to me, "We need you to go buy us some beer."

"Sorry, we're just about to sit down for dinner." I was nervous about how they would respond.

My suspicion confirmed, the ringleader said, "Just so you know, if you don't do it, you can't drive around with us anymore." (Since I was the youngest of the group, I did not have a car or a *real* driver's license yet.)

It was blackmail and felt so wrong, but I agreed anyhow. They picked me up, I bought their beer, and they dropped me back off at the Carpenter's house. I'm sure I came up with some lame excuse as to why I had to leave just as dinner was being served. Telling the truth must have felt too shameful. I had lost my voice because I did not want to be the bad slut again—I wanted to be their friend and I guess I felt I had to prove myself.

As an adult, I now understand bullying. Control and criticism are a bully's favorite tools. Adults who control or harm someone through judgment and criticism are really just grown up schoolyard bullies. It looks different later in life, but it's not. My friends' criticism after "the kiss" turned into self-criticism, which became the catalyst for my allowing them to control me and my time. It all began with criticism.

Criticism often begins as a passive internal judgment and then turns into active externalization. There is usually nothing positive about criticism, because it is not often about feedback, support, or lifting someone up. It is usually about power. Unless we are evaluating with love and with the purpose of building someone up, pondering and pointing out perceived faults is highly critical. It's judging someone's thoughts, words, or actions as being bad—not just wrong, because being wrong is simply about making a mistake. We all make mistakes. Loving corrections are excellent learning opportunities. Interestingly though, often people criticize because they are projecting their own faults and insecurities onto others. *This* is bad.

PROJECTION

Steven Ozanich wrote in his powerful book, *The Great Pain Deception*, "We innately know we are conflicted when we attempt to avoid admitting any conflict by casting our shadow, or undesirable qualities, onto others in what is called **projection**. We use projection to reduce our personal anxiety by slipping our own personal flaws past our egos—making us feel good about ourselves by judging and criticizing others—whose faults are simply our own faults that we deny. The other guy always has the problems, so if she can convince herself of this, she feels better about herself by 'bringing down' others, assuaging her own guilt and low self-esteem."

If you find yourself continually judging people, Anil Gupta suggests in his book, *Immediate Happiness,* that you write down your judgmental thoughts. He says, "I still have them and so do you." Yes, it's okay to admit it—we all have them. But rather than voicing them, why not purge them from your brain, put them down on paper, and then take a good hard look at them. This alone can remove the power from the thoughts.

On the other hand, if the judgment is still acute, try using the technique Byron Katie teaches in her book, *Loving What Is.* She suggests asking yourself the following four questions when faced with personally judging or criticizing someone or something:

1. "Is it true?" For example, let's say we think that our mate should be spending more time with us, we would ask ourselves something like, "Is it true that my mate should spend more time with me?" Yes or no. If no, move to question #3.

2. "Can I *absolutely* know that it's true?" Yes or no. Most everything will be a no, as we really can't know the *absolute* truth about anything. Who dictated that a relationship should look a certain way with a prescribed amount of hours together or apart? How can we *absolutely* know that our thoughts are correct—I should be getting more time with my mate—and theirs are wrong—they need more time for personal recreation? The truth might be that I should be developing better relationships with other friends and family members, as he really does need more guy time for his wellbeing. Get the point?

3. Then ask yourself, "How do I react when I believe that [negative] thought?" Really ponder this intently. Do you feel cranky? Unloved? Mad? Resentful? Consider who you BECOME when you think those thoughts? Do you withhold love? Are you full of anxiety? Does life seem like a battle? Is your marriage suffering? When you judge another's supposed faults, your reactions are creating more faults within yourself. How can you be the highest and best version of you with this level of mental toxicity?

4. Lastly, ask, "Who would I be *without* that [negative] thought?" Wouldn't you be someone totally different? Someone full of compassion and understanding? Someone more joyful? If you thought something like, "I'm grateful my husband is so passionate about his hobbies. It makes our time together much more energized! Imagine if I was his only source of entertainment? Yikes." See how that's such a different place to live? Thoughts truly can change your reality.

The next time critical thoughts cascade through your mind, try to get clear about the truth of the matter. The person, organization, or situation is rarely the problem—it's usually your thinking. Maybe the person is simply different than you. Maybe you just need to give up your expectations for others to be perfect. Maybe your view on what constitutes correct behavior or the 'right' way to live is just a personal preference with which you are attempting to burden another. Instead, gift them with freedom from criticism—it's a much lighter load for you both.

WHY DO WE JUDGE AND CRITICIZE?

The great philosophers Sigmund Freud and Carl Jung both concluded that we judge and criticize because our ego and our super ego are at war. We want to look good on the outside, while still harboring a hidden shadow side. This conflict is way too uncomfortable, so we become masters at projection. As mentioned earlier, rather than admitting any dark side within, we choose to project our undesirable qualities onto others. Another way of saying this is, "If you spot it, you've got it." Or, "For every one finger that's pointed outward, there are three fingers pointed back at me." (Try it...you'll get the visual.)

Projection is an interesting thing to ponder and personally helps me avoid the temptation to judge and criticize others. If I can see a trait in someone else that I don't particularly like, I can, with a fairly high level of certainty, know that I have that trait also. This helps me shut my mouth, change my thoughts, and have compassion for that person as well as for myself. I can mindfully summon gratitude, as he or she is a gift to me—a mirror through which I can see my own need for healing or growth in a certain area. This is a much more joyful way of living than empowering the bitterness that comes from walking in judgment.

Before I'm tempted to criticize another, I ask myself, "What part of my shadow self is being touched right now? Where do I need to grow and change? How can I walk in compassion rather than criticism?"

Commit to keeping your eye on the target—you. As the late Wayne Dyer said, "When you judge another, you do not define them, you define yourself."

Exercise #3: A Transformational Game

Personal judgment is the precursor to criticism. The key to controlling criticism is to nip it in the bud at the judgment stage before it even becomes criticism. And remember that criticism can be spoken or unspoken—both are equally damaging. To be a Safe Soul, be diligent in catching yourself in the personal judgment stage. Even make a game of it. Notice when you are personally judging someone in your thoughts and then decide to intentionally shift them.

Taking a thought and turning it on its head will change our attitudes, our ability to love, and our own personal happiness. Here are some examples:

Thought: "Wow, does Joe dress like a slob."

Shift: "How refreshing to see someone not so caught up in his looks."

Thought: "It's so frustrating that Helen's always late. She clearly has no respect for others."

Shift: "Maybe Helen's in overwhelm. I'm going to ask if there's anything I can do to alleviate some of her stress." Or, "I'm going to have a clear and private conversation with Helen to let her know that her tardiness is affecting her work. I'll ask if there is anything I can do to help her become someone who is consistently on time or even early."

Thought: "Holy cow! Mark's a jerk."

Shift: "I wonder what's going on in Mark's world that makes him act like that. I'm going to take him for a drink and see how I can support him."

Thought: "Gawd! What hideous makeup. Why the need for all that face paint?"

Shift: "I just love seeing the diversity of humanity. How boring it would be if we were all the same!"

Get the idea? You can literally make it a game to see how much you can shift your thoughts. It will change your life. It will have you be a glass-half-full type. It will cause you to be a nicer and better person. Your businesses and relationships will transform and grow exponentially. Try it!

Now, if you just can't find *anything* good to say about someone or something, do as Joel Osteen says, "If you cannot be positive, then at least be quiet."

A personal caveat to this quote: check in with yourself—dig deep to determine why you cannot find anything positive to say. Is it something to do with them or is it something inside of you? Are you holding onto negative feelings or thoughts about the person? Do you need to actively purge anything from your thinking? Do you need to have a Clearing Conversation? (See pp.91,92.)

CHAPTER 5

THE PERFECT STORM

It's much more valuable to look for strength in others.
You gain nothing by criticizing their imperfections.

~ Daisaku Ikeda

Each of the arenas—gossip, triangulation, and criticism—can be problematic on their own, but when they are combined, their sum has even more destructive power than each does individually.

A TRIFECTA

Gossip, triangulation, and criticism are incredibly common and insidious—even among the 'spiritually evolved.'

I was at a dinner party recently and was enjoying a great time giggling and chatting with two wonderful women. Both were leaders in their churches, conference keynote speakers, prayer ministers, etc. Throughout the night, we talked about a lot of lovely ideas, experiences, things, and people. They shared the topics of their upcoming retreats, the service they were doing in their communities, some ideas for future work possibilities, and the like. It was a nurturing time and we connected well.

Then it derailed into the unsafe zone. The men retired into the living room to watch the playoff hockey game and the three of us gals went to the kitchen to clean up and make dessert. (I know, this sounds terribly cliché, but this is how it went down.)

Then one of the women started going on about a co-worker of

hers. "Do you know Marcia is the ONLY teacher in the whole school not doing a field trip to the zoo this fall? I mean, she never goes above and beyond, EVER. And it's so easy to do a field trip. You enlist a few volunteer parents, get the waivers signed, and away you go! When she came to me about it, I had so much to say, but all I did was remain quiet and give her *the look*." (She lowered her chin and raised one eyebrow like a mother might do to guilt trip a child.) She continued, "It's so disappointing. Marcia just needs to step up!"

I was surprised by this sudden change of character and instantly lost a little of my respect for her. I also felt like this isn't a person I would trust with my soul. Her words might seem minor—not a big deal—but there are a number of unsafe things going on here.

Firstly, she was *gossiping*. It was pure idle chatter at the expense of another.

Secondly, she was *triangulating*. She could have simply gone straight to her colleague with compassion rather than airing her disappointment to someone completely removed from the scenario. She might have said to her colleague, "Hey, I notice you've been overwhelmed with all the extracurricular activities lately. I know it must feel like a lot. Is there anyway I can help you, especially with the field trip to the zoo? The kids would really enjoy it. I'd love to take that off your plate if necessary." This could have totally altered the course of events, whereas triangulating did nothing but solidify the grievance.

Thirdly, she was *criticizing*. She had no idea what was going on in her co-worker's class that had Marcia decide to forgo the field trip. She also had no idea what was occurring in her world that had her overwhelmed to the point of only being able to commit to the basic responsibilities of teaching.

It was a trifecta of GTC—a perfect, horrible storm of negativity.

In my typical stick-up-for-the-underdog mode, I lovingly (I hope) interjected. "Perhaps there's a good reason why Marcia can't take the kids to the zoo. Maybe she's in complete overwhelm and that event would just put her over the top? Since you said it's really easy to organize, maybe you could suggest that you'd like to take it on? Could you tell her you'd love to help in this way?" Hmmm, what a concept? Her wheels were spinning.

While I didn't pull out the whole Safe Souls distinction manual and have a workshop right there in the kitchen, I simply modeled a different way of being and offered suggestions. This had her self-convicted. She went quiet and I could see her mind was in motion. Then the other gal chimed in lovingly and started offering other suggestions and also began defending her friend's co-worker as well. Beautiful!

The point of sharing this story is not to make anyone wrong. Unfortunately, it's our culture. People gossip. People triangulate. People criticize. This example just happened to involve all three. Here was this fabulous woman—a leader in the church, a nurturing mother, an adoring wife, a vivacious presence, and a keynote speaker at huge conferences about God's love and grace—yet she had no idea she was not exhibiting these qualities herself in this instance. She was not 'doing unto others as you would have them do unto you' and she was not upholding the commandment to 'not judge, lest you be judged.' These are Biblical quotes with which she would be very familiar. I hope she realized she was not being what she was teaching, so she could course-correct and fully walk-the-talk.

I love a status update that my friend Joey Robert Parks recently wrote. It encapsulates the effect of letting go of judgment. "I've finally learned to take all my loneliness and anxiety and direct it toward things that can benefit from it (my fiction writing). The result is replacing the void with LOVE. Lots of LOVE. The unconditional kind. The non-judgmental kind. I never realized how much I used to judge people until I had an 'ah-ha' moment and learned to accept and love people as they are. It's so freeing." That's the truth. Freedom comes from walking in love rather than judgment. Try it.

Author and speaker, Brené Brown, Ph.D., shares that, "Connection is the energy that is created between people when they feel seen, heard, and valued; when they can give and receive without judgment."

These elevated levels of love, connection, and freedom are my dream for the planet.

NO ONE IS IMMUNE

The trifecta story I just shared shows that GTC can affect anyone anywhere, even spiritual leaders and places you would not expect it to be prevalent. Because GTC can happen anywhere, Safe Souls can be implemented everywhere. We are all human and beautifully flawed. If willing, we can learn and grow through our imperfection. We can also use our free will and a filter of love to give respect to others, even those who oppose our views.

Once you become aware of how insidious gossip, triangulation, and criticism are, you will start catching yourself GTC'ing regularly. It can happen while talking to your boss at work, or to someone in your place of worship, or even to your best friend. When you find yourself falling into that trap, you have an immediate opportunity to evoke Safe Souls.

You can say something like, "Frank, I just don't feel right talking about Susan behind her back. Can we make a promise to one another to refrain from that? Can we agree to only discuss Susan's business when she is with us and can participate in the conversation?"

It is really that simple to do. It's not even necessary to make Safe Souls a formal signed agreement, as you might in a company or large institution. It can easily be an informal, verbal promise you make one-on-one with someone close to you. Because it is aligned with positive behavior, most anyone would agree. If they do not agree, then you may want to reassess the relationship you have with that particular person.

STORMS DON'T JUST HAPPEN

Storms take time to form; they are not instant processes. Evaporation occurs and, if certain environmental conditions prevail, a storm cloud will ensue. With the proper wind strength and direction, as well as air pressure, the storm begins to move toward a destination. A perfect storm arises when these conditions occur simultaneously in different locations, forming one large, unstoppable force. These perfect storms are destructive and leave a swath of ruins in their wake.

In business and in life, the three storm clouds of gossip, triangulation, and criticism can occur simultaneously, can include a multitude of people, and can destroy a company, family, or group of friends if early intervention is not implemented. There is a silver lining here: an actual environmental storm cannot be stopped—we just don't have that level of scientific technology—but using the philosophical technology outlined in Safe Souls, we can avoid the formation of many devastating interpersonal tornados.

CHANGING THE NORM

Companies have their own ethos—the way people act, interact, and treat one another. Behaviors are dictated by these cultural norms. For instance, if you work in a casual environment, it may be acceptable to wear jeans and a t-shirt to work. A new hire can quickly see clues signifying the corporate culture. In order to assimilate, he will often attempt to look like, talk like, and act like his counterparts.

This process is common, normal, and is a way one might try to feel a part of the culture. Conformity has another purpose, however, and it is one based on fear—if you do not conform you will be on the outside. You worry that others will turn against you or, in the worst circumstance, that you will be fired.

Healthy interpersonal etiquette, the kind Safe Souls offers, provides a way to conform to positive ideals and behaviors.

Sometimes, however, it does not seem possible—cultures can be so toxic that the people operating within them can't see through the smog. Kind, clean, and clear communication throughout the community can appear unattainable. You might be faced with the following or similar situations and could feel like you're the only one trying to affect change by being a stand for Safe Souls. Stepping up might feel lonely and, in some cases, may even put your job at risk. But we encourage you to step out boldly and do the right thing. You will be a better person for it.

- If someone repeats an off-color or racist joke, do you laugh at it to conform? Or do you make a stand for what is right?

- If someone ridicules a co-worker and everyone else joins in, do you follow suit? Or do you stand up for him and become the odd person out?

- If your co-workers talk about how bad the boss's ideas are as soon as she leaves the room, do you agree? Or do you defend her?

Of course we would all like to say we would do the right thing, but we have found that most people will either remain silent or join in, not because they are bad people, but because they do not want to alienate themselves or those around them. They do not want to be accused of being a killjoy, of seeming 'holier than thou,' or of not being a team player. They may also not want to embarrass the person by calling out his less than gracious comments.

This is why a company's leadership should set the standards and implement Safe Souls both personally and corporately. This not only fosters a more positive culture, it also gives people permission to speak up if GTC is occurring, without fear of retaliation. Engaging in GTC will become an unacceptable cultural practice as Safe Souls becomes the corporate norm. And it can be beautifully self-governing if everyone is on board.

NORMS GONE BAD

In the news recently there have been many stories in which one bully, or even groups of bullies, are doing horrible things to their classmates. Onlookers are plentiful and videographers are hopeful to capture a YouTube upload that goes viral, but those who take a stand are becoming increasingly scarce. Sometimes bullying can go on for months or even years without anyone breaking the silence.

Sociologists and behavioral scientists studying this phenomenon found that those who joined the instigating bully and participated in the malicious acts said they felt if they abandoned or confronted the bully, they could become the next victim. Also, the bullies may have been the victims of prior bullies, and so bullying another becomes their rite of passage. Upper classman have reported they sometimes felt it was their duty to bully and hurt their younger compatriots because it was done to them.

What about the passive bystanders—those who didn't actively engage, but still watched the abuse? They reported that they did not want to be a snitch. They did not want to be the odd person out, to be ridiculed, or worse, to be harmed themselves. So the pattern of destructive behavior continues. The bystanders and victims often cite 'helplessness' to do or say anything because they felt this was just normal in their club, sports team, or school. The worst part of these stories is that often coaches or teachers knew what was occurring, but did nothing. They felt this was just natural behavior. 'Boys will be boys!'

Bullying does not necessarily stop at high school—it occurs with adults—and often begins with GTC going unchecked. Safe Souls will not change everyone, but it does put bullies on notice. Either they conform to the new set of standards, or they are respectfully shown the door. Those that do not adapt to a more positive culture will have no place there and their removal will create a happier and safer environment for those who do embrace the healthier ethos. They are not being rejected; they are rejecting the Safe Souls lifestyle themselves.

We have seen this happen in a half a dozen situations over the years. Some bad apples were destroying a healthy culture. A few were at work, some were in our circle of friends, and others were even family members. Painful as it was, once we, as gently as possible, removed the bullies, each culture flourished because safety was restored. We were often thanked profusely for having the courage to perform the painful surgery of removing the unsafe souls. A few times those who didn't understand the toxicity of the situation criticized us, but we stood by our values and peace ensued. Invariably things thrive in a healthy environment.

If others can't conform to Safe Souls' distinct and healthy boundaries and you need to remove them from your inner circle, remember—hindsight is always 20/20 while courage to change things is not. Removing them may seem hard and even harsh, but sometimes we need to step out in our convictions, without the benefit of a crystal clear visual, for change to occur. If we do it with kindness and integrity, the outcome will eventually be positive.

In the next few chapters, you will learn how to practically implement Safe Souls and thus avoid the pitfalls created by gossip, triangulation, and criticism. You will be able change destructive habits before they obliterate your organization, home, or circle of friends from the inside out.

Exercise #4: Cleaning Up the Past

Take two minutes to list a few specific situations where you have gossiped, triangulated, or criticized. Then commit to a Clearing Conversation around each instance. (See pp.91,92.) Schedule a time to apologize and have a kind, open, heart-to-heart conversation with the person or people involved. Use the SOAP technique and invite everyone to share his or her feelings around the situation as well.

A few caveats to consider: if a conversation would harm another, do not have it. Also, your truth can be used inadvertently as a weapon, so consider your audience and what the outcome might be. Lastly, check your motivation for having the conversation— it is not only to clear your conscience, it is primarily to build another up.

Consider how you felt when you were gossiping, triangulating, or criticizing? Don't beat yourself up. Today is a new day and your actions going forward can be totally different than they were yesterday.

_____

_____

_____

_____

_____

_____

_____

_____

_____

_____

_____

_____

_____

_____

CHAPTER 6

TOOLS FOR TRANSFORMATION

Constant criticism kills love...kindness helps
it blossom and grow.

~ Debra Roberts

In addition to the basic formula of Safe Souls—No GTC—and to the easy-to-recall acronyms of THINK and SOAP—there are four main 'Tools for Transformation' that can help you flex the Safe Souls muscle within every interaction, no matter the relationship.

These four tools provide you with new ways to communicate that not only show respect to an individual, but foster trust and compassion as well.

1. Clearing Conversations
These conversations help clear the air and leave nothing unspoken or lingering. Everyone walks away being heard, understood, and ultimately healed. Souls are left intact. In fact, why not go beyond leaving souls simply intact and leave each person feeling genuinely loved and empowered?

2. Committed Conversations for Action
These strategic conversations with a safe third party are meant to reduce the possibility of a poor Clearing Conversation outcome. If a person feels he is in an overly heightened emotional state and the conversation could do more harm than good, it is sometimes wise to first bounce thoughts off of a

neutral third party. The caveat is that the Safe Soul sounding board must get a commitment by the one with the complaint that she will ultimately have a Clearing Conversation with her colleague, friend, partner, or with whomever she had the conflict.

3. Covering People's Backs

This is a gracious way of operating. If we all have each other's backs in conversation, it ensures that No GTC will occur. It is not only a commitment to refraining from GTC personally, but when you encounter it happening with others, you promise to address it and shift the discussion to positive conversations and praise. When people know their backs are covered, they can avoid the fight, flight, or freeze modes—they can be free to love, to create, to self-actualize. Social harmony will ensue.

4. Public/Private Praise

Both public and private praise are needed and are such elegant ways of operating. They perform different functions—with public praise, we are encouraged to praise in the company of others. The energy, excitement, and love this type of praise generates is palpable. It can even cause people who may not have seen praiseworthy traits in someone suddenly see the light. Private praise is more intimate. It can really help solidify and grow relationships between two people.

The following is a deeper dive into each tool.

I. CLEARING CONVERSATIONS

One of my favorite Tools for Transformation is the Clearing Conversation. I have found it to be one of the toughest, but most rewarding practices I've implemented.

Have you ever just *known* that something was up with someone? That the energy between you was not clean and clear? That there were unspoken words and emotions swirling? I think we all have. And what do you do with that tension? Ignore it? Avoid the person? Brush it off? What if that person is directly in your world and you have to be in his presence often? Or what if he's in the periphery of your life, but you still want to live above such muck and mire? You can have a simple Clearing Conversation.

This is such a basic discipline—it feels a bit like suggesting you brush your teeth at night—but, unfortunately, it's not a commonly practiced one. It is uncommon because it can be scary. It can leave us feeling vulnerable. We don't know how the person is going to react once we share with them our suspicions—that there is something negative between us. But I can tell you that 98% of the hundreds of Clearing Conversations I've had have gone extremely well. The exceptions have been with those who just can't dig deep, get vulnerable, be real with their emotions, and commit to a higher way. It's sad when they go wrong, but when they go right, they are magical.

REALTOR JOE

We were in the process of buying a new house in Phoenix and were using a recommended realtor to help us. He had our wish list—a view, within walking distance to the Camelback corridor, and a highly contemporary design. The first two items were virtually mutually exclusive—to get a view, you need to be way up the hill—and the last item is almost impossible to find in Phoenix. So Joe had only shown us about 3 homes in our 6 months of actively looking. It was not for lack of trying—there was just no inventory. Being a former realtor in Vancouver myself, I did most of the footwork—searched properties on MLS, did drive-bys, and went to open houses. So Joe and I had not really developed the normal broker/buyer relationship; we had spent virtually no time together. And herein lay the issue.

His communication, mainly by text and email, started to become a bit sharper, less jovial. If he were an emoticon user, I would say that the smiley faces ceased. I reacted by pulling away to protect myself. This went on for a few weeks and then deteriorated even further right in the thick of negotiating on a great little Al Beadle home we had fallen in love with. Each communication provided a cortisol zing.

I had no idea what was happening in the background. I had closed hundreds of millions of dollars worth of real estate deals during my former career and this was the worst feeling transaction with which I'd been involved. When I was assisting a buyer or a seller or both, my goal was always a win-win-win—buyer wins, seller wins, broker wins. This is a joyful start to living in a new home, a happy way to sell a property, and perfect career insurance—you will surely be used in each person's future real estate transactions if you can pull off a win-win-win.

Our deal was definitely not occurring this way and we had come to a bit of a stalemate. I felt the sellers were being stubborn on a few minor terms, we were about $25,000 apart on the price, and it seemed that Joe wasn't going to bat for us. (He was double ending the deal—meaning he was representing both the buyers and the sellers.)

It was interesting timing because earlier that week I had been to a Toastmasters meeting and the speaker was a lawyer talking about the art of negotiations. During the presentation, he made a comment that lawyers are notoriously poor negotiators because they are generally very black and white—they are used to the law being the law with no wiggle room. Could THIS be the problem? Joe was an ex-litigator.

Back to the impasse.

After witnessing my frustration, Ken said, "Just get the deal done and move on. The added stress is not worth $25,000 and a few inclusions." But the impasse in our negotiation was not really the issue—the energy in our communications was. THAT was causing the stress. It did not feel safe. So I called Joe and asked him if we could meet for a quick coffee. We planned it for the next day.

The conversation went like this:

I said, "Joe, I feel like something has derailed. Buying a home is supposed to be one of the most exciting times and this has been feeling very heavy. I'm not sure if the sellers are being super stubborn or if you're not stepping up for us, or maybe a bit of both? But I feel like we have made huge concessions and they haven't. I'm almost ready to walk away because I believe that if things don't start well, they rarely end well. Buying this home should be joyful, and it isn't. Is there something I've done to annoy you? It just feels like something's in the space of our relationship—it's not clean and clear."

"I'm so glad you brought this up, Lori. I've been feeling similar things. I think it goes back to the snippy email you sent about my search parameters."

Yikes. "Really? Tell me more," I said.

He continued, "Well, when your friend sent you information about that home for sale on East Marston, you sent me a snippy email asking what my plan was for finding us a home. You wrote that the East Marston listing had all the criteria—view, walkable, and contemporary—so why had you not suggested we see it?"

I could feel my eyes well up. He was totally misinterpreting the email. What was more—my very core, the essence of who I am, was being misunderstood.

I was shocked. "Oh my gosh, Joe, I'm so sorry it came off that way. That was TOTALLY not my intention. I was just asking the question so nothing got missed. Honestly. Please go back and re-read the email with a view that I was in no way even thinking snippy thoughts let alone writing them. I think you'll see that my email was not accusatory. I was just seeking information."

He said, "Wow, really? I totally thought you were judging my professionalism and performance. Another thing that bothered me was when I suggested you drive by that architecturally significant 'cube' house and Ken dissed it. I could hear him in the background saying that we are so far off on our communications of what we're looking for. It was harsh."

Ah ha! These were the issues. There WAS something in the space that was causing tension, fear, and anxiety. And it took a Clearing Conversation to unearth it. The interaction shifted from fear and anxiety to love and grace. We both saw how, through email especially, things can get misconstrued. We both talked about how much we appreciated and respected each other and how much fun it had been at the beginning. I told Joe that I really liked him and would love to develop a longer-term professional relationship. It was a very empowering conversation. We had gotten to the bottom of the negative energy and we had shifted it.

"I wish I had spoken up right away when those things bothered me," Joe said.

"Me too, but I'm glad we had this chance to clear the air." Hugs followed.

Then he got up from the table and said, "I'm going to get you the price and the inclusions you are asking for." And he did.

NO BOOZE FOR A YOGINI

Another example was a Clearing Conversation I had the other day with a girlfriend. It was probably unnecessary for her, but from my level of commitment to Safe Souls, it was essential for me.

I had set her up with a friend, but after a few dates, she said she wasn't interested. "He drinks too much and then gets goofy," she shared. Being a young mom, a yogini, and having a commitment to a super healthy lifestyle, she's not a drinker at all. But he was smitten.

When he probed as to why she was not interested, I told him that she's just super healthy and not into going out dining and drinking all the time. I added, "She also said you can get a little goofy when you drink." Whoops! As soon as the words were out, I knew I shouldn't have spoken them. There was a defensive voice inside of me that said, 'wait a minute; she never told you that in confidence.' Regardless, I had shared something that didn't need to be shared. It did not feel right because it could have made him feel bad and it could have caused dissention in their friendship. And my comment certainly didn't pass the THINK test.

I decided to have a Clearing Conversation with her. I told her that I said something super stupid to Vince—that she was not interested in him because he gets goofy when he drinks. I told her I felt like I had gossiped, triangulated, and broken a confidence and that I was sorry.

She laughed and said, "No worries! I had already told him the same thing." I felt better for telling her, and it did not matter whether she had told him or not, or that it did not bother her, because it bothered me. I felt better for coming clean.

They stopped seeing each other for a while, but we recently saw them together. They said they were on a date and were taking things slowly. Because I had cleared the air with her, when I saw them at the restaurant, I could approach them with complete clarity and love. There was nothing I had to worry about. I had no thoughts such as, "Did he tell her what I had said? Was she mad at me for saying it? Were they talking about the stupid words I had spoken?" There was nothing but love and respect in the space between us. A Clearing Conversation allowed me to be free of shame.

II. COMMITTED CONVERSATIONS FOR ACTION

What do we do if we have a personal conflict, but fear we are too emotionally charged to go right to the individual about it? How do we best process this anxiety?

There are many strategies. We can stop, breathe, and meditate about it. We can journal about it. We can hire a professional coach to discuss it. We can send loving thoughts to the person. There are countless things we can do to ease the conflict until we are ready for a discussion. But what if our feelings are just too intense? What if we feel the need to confide in another human being before having a Clearing Conversation with the actual person?

Everyone should have a handful of Safe Souls in their arsenal with whom they can discuss personal and confidential matters at any time. It is with these people that we can have what we call a Committed Conversation for Action.

A caveat is this: unless your workmates, family members, or playmates are operating at a very high level of Safe Souls, or are flexing the muscle to do so, the Safe Soul you enlist should be someone in another circle. In a best-case scenario, the Safe Soul should not even know the person with whom you are having the conflict. Otherwise it could be stepping into the zone of GTC and you could also be tainting one's opinion of another unnecessarily.

For example, if your grievance is with a person at work and you are having trouble formulating the Clearing Conversation, you might decide to approach a fellow workmate for a Committed Conversation for Action. In this case, you will inevitably bring some negative things about the other into the discussion, i.e., the issue you are having with her behavior. The listener may have never even noticed these traits in the person, but now that you've raised them, they might suddenly be glaring. Now you have caused division and further decay in the organization. Same within a family—if one brother has an issue with another brother, and goes to a third brother for a Committed Conversation for Action, the third brother will naturally be filled with the speaker's opinions. If he is operating at a high level of Safe Souls, he will be able to give some good advice, be a catalyst for a Clearing Conversation, and ultimately used for good. But if he is not operating as a Safe Soul, division could ensue.

If, however, your workplace, your family, or your friends are committed to Safe Souls, having a Committed Conversation for Action with someone in the same arena can be incredibly bonding and healing. When there is a lot at stake and two people come together out of love and concern to solve an issue, it can create a synergy that was not present before the conversation. Diving deeply into a difficult conversation and inviting those around you to do the same can be a growth opportunity for an organization, a family, and a group of friends. It can catapult everyone into a new level of operating. But make sure that it is a Committed Conversation for Action with the intent of conflict resolution and leaving everyone's soul intact and even enriched.

To be clear, a Committed Conversation for Action is one in which the following occurs:

1. The speaker enlists his Safe Soul confidant to speak about the anxiety-producing situation privately. The Safe Soul, by her very nature, will not allow gossip, triangulation, or criticism, but will suggest inviting the person into the conversation immediately. They will call in the third party and have a Clearing Conversation to resolve the issue. All parties should be left feeling heard, loved, and empowered. Their souls will be intact.

2. If the speaker says that he needs to process with the Safe Soul first before having the Clearing Conversation with the person, that's okay, but only with the commitment that he will bring the grievance to the person as soon as possible after this current discussion. If that condition cannot be met, the Safe Soul should not listen to the person's grievance.

An amendment to the above is something I recently stumbled upon. It was unexpected, and I think it fits beautifully into Safe Souls. I was having a Committed Conversation for Action with one of my Safe Soul girlfriends, Cathie, about an offense that had recently occurred. I wasn't sure how to address the person without offending her or being overly reactive. When I took Cathie through the details, they became increasingly ridiculous. As I spoke the words, healing was occurring, my resentment was lifting, and I was seeing my part in it all. It became clear to me that it was not even a can of worms, let alone a can of worms I should open. Since Cathie was not judging my conversation or trying to 'fix' anything, I was able to talk through it and see clearly that the issue rested solely within me. I took responsibility for my stinkin' thinkin' and ended the conversation with a number of praises for my other friend.

In this case, I weighed the pros and cons of ultimately having a Clearing Conversation with the other person and felt that I would actually be a safer soul by NOT having one than I would by having one. I was in the wrong, not her, so why even waste a moment of energy going through it?

James Pennebaker, Ph.D., suggests in his book, *Opening Up: The Healing Power of Confiding in Others,* that the key to good confiding is in choosing the confidant and that the most important factor is trust. Beyond that, you should find someone who will not judge or criticize you and who is a safe or anonymous listener. If you don't want to risk even vocalizing your grievance—write down all the things that anger you and simply throw them away.

THE DANCE OF PARTNERSHIP CONFERENCE

At a two-day conference a few years ago, we were put into trios to share what came up for each of us during the previous teaching segment. The ground rules were simple: 1) each person got two full minutes to share, and 2) they were not to be interrupted or counseled by the others during, or even after, their share. It was to be a safe place to open our souls and process the contents.

About halfway through my sharing, one of the ladies cut me off and made a pretty dismissive and harsh comment about how I should just do this and that and proceeded to give her opinion on how I should handle the situation about which I was sharing. Wow. Okay, first off, I was not looking for any counsel. Secondly, it was my turn to share. Thirdly, did she not hear the ground rules!? After my slight shock, I interrupted her and gently said, "I wasn't looking for advice or opinions, I'm just sharing what came up for me and would appreciate if you stuck with the ground rules and just listened." She stopped talking, seemingly taken aback that I had stood my ground and enforced the boundaries.

For the rest of the day I avoided this lady. Just looking at her triggered something in me. She looked so mean. A fairly permanent scowl donned her face and her body language wasn't exactly 'come and hug me.' She rarely seemed to smile. So I resigned myself to just staying far away from her for the rest of the weekend. And with fifty women at the conference, that would have been fairly easy.

But the whole scenario bugged me. The space was not clean and clear in the room. There was this rope of negative energy from me to her and from her to me and it ate away at my peace.

So I decided to clean it up. But before doing so, I needed some advice. I went to one of my Safe Soul sisters in the workshop, described the situation, and got some input. Normally, I would just go up to the person and clear the air, but in this case I was actually afraid of her. She triggered something in me and I needed some support. And I wanted to make sure my emotionally heightened state didn't do more harm than good.

After processing my anxiety with Caitlyn, I went up to the lady—her name was Wendy—and asked if we could talk. She said she had to get up to her hotel room and that she was really tired. Part of me thought, 'Phew, well I made the effort, I guess I'm off the hook if she doesn't want to receive it.' But the bigger part of me pressed, saying it would just take a minute.

She agreed, reluctantly.

I was sweating.

I said, "Wendy, I've been avoiding you all day and I'm sorry. When you interrupted and advised me during my share, it triggered something. I felt dishonored, unheard, and unsafe. I don't even know you, but I've been rejecting you all afternoon since. I'm sure you're a great human and I'm sorry I've been avoiding you. Can you forgive me?"

You can't believe how her face softened. Tears welled up in her eyes and she went on to tell me her story.

She was eastern European and when she came to the States as a youngster she was ostracized. Girls had been incredibly mean to her, so she had spent her life in a stance of defense and protection. I could see it. Her body language spoke clearly. She had a view that everyone was out to get her. She wore a prickly demeanor so that no one could even get close, let alone hurt her further.

The beauty of this interaction was not only that I had stepped through my fear and insecurity and had honored her by sharing how I was essentially being an unsafe soul (by avoiding her, judging her, and overreacting to how she treated me), the net result was that I had given her a huge gift without even knowing it. The next day she went to the front of the conference during an open sharing opportunity, took the microphone, and proceeded to speak about how that interaction had her see that she had been operating out of fear her whole life, that she got to experience and receive my love, and saw that not all women are mean. That's how she had viewed 50% of the population her entire life—women were the enemy.

A simple Safe Souls Committed Conversation for Action followed by a heartfelt Clearing Conversation, delivered in love, freed her forever.

III. COVERING PEOPLE'S BACKS

Trust is formed when we know someone has our back. It is the feeling of security and safety we have when we step outside a room, certain that those we leave behind have our best interest at heart.

Have you ever left a room and felt unsafe afterwards? You sensed that the people were immediately talking about you when you departed? Conversely, having someone's back means that when they leave the room, you will fight for their soul if others are trying to sabotage them. Having someone's back also means that they can confide in you knowing their proclamation will be kept private. Having someone's back means that when the chips are down you will be there to support, love, and even defend them.

For example, if an unsafe soul says, "Gosh, since he has become financially successful, he thinks he's God's gift to the planet. Do you see how he drives around in his fancy new car?"

A Safe Soul friend will respond with something like, "Really, I don't think he feels that way or intentionally flaunts his success at all. Wouldn't you love to trade in your rust bucket for a solid new set of wheels if you had the money? We should be excited for him. In fact, did you know that he gives away thousands every month to a homeless charity? And he's quite aware how his success might hinder his long-term friendships and is doing everything he can to stop that from happening."

How easy it might have been for him to have a knee-jerk reaction and just say, "Yeah, I agree." But how much lovelier it was for him to honor his friend and defend his character in his absence.

Do you have people like that in your life? Are you that somebody for a friend, family member, or work mate?

I hope I was for my friend Cam in the following scenario.

SNICKERING SALESPEOPLE

I walked into the following conversation a number of years ago while selling a 175-unit real estate project in British Columbia. We had produced a stellar pre-launch campaign and had virtually every condominium reserved by potential buyers prior to the official launch, scheduled for the next day.

"What the hell does Cam think he's doing? What an idiot. We've worked so hard to create this campaign, to excite our prospect list, and to build momentum, and now this!? Raising prices at the eleventh hour? It's so unfair!" said one team member.

"I know. This is ridiculous. A 10% increase across the board? It's complete bullshit," said another.

While I was not surprised at the first person's comments—he had a tendency to vocalize his frustrations—I was surprised by my other colleague's response. She was such a solid person and was always on-board and encouraging through any change in campaign. She really did want what was best for each project. Since it was out of character for her, I chalked it up to fatigue, frustration, and peer-pressure. None of us are perfect and this was not her normal way of being. This also shows how one bad apple can easily ruin the pie if we are not diligent with our commitment to Safe Souls.

The 'idiot' they were referring to, in addition to being my friend, was our broker and the owner of the real estate marketing company where we all hung our real estate licenses. He had risked his own time, capital, and reputation to build a company through which we were all making huge incomes. He deserved better.

To me it seemed obvious—if people were throwing deposit checks at us that fast and furiously, we had left money on the table. Prices were set too low. There is always a risky sweet spot to pricing a development just beyond what we think we can actually achieve. Then we have to step up our sales skills and make it happen. It was our job to maximize our client's profits. (Our clients were not really the buyers, though we did act on their behalf, they were the real estate developers whose projects we sold.)

We were a highly sought after, award-winning sales and marketing team, and had done an incredible job of building the momentum, excitement, and purchase commitments, but at the last minute some of my colleagues did not seem to want to work for a living. They seemed to want to take Easy Street. How much more fun would it be to actually blow the client away with sales figures that far surpassed what their pro-formas predicted?

Maybe they were just tired.

"Hey guys. Let's not head into our launch tomorrow with all this negative energy and thinking, okay?" As the Sales Manager for the project, this was my responsibility to say. But even more so, as Cam's friend, it was my duty to cover his back. He was doing the right thing by raising the prices and we needed to support him on that decision. Nattering about it was not helpful or kind.

My opinion was not popular with everyone. But I stood firm, asked them to get into a gratitude mindset for the opportunity to sell this development, and suggested they quickly get on board with the new pricing. My commissions on that three-month job were about $125K, so I was not going to whine about anything. More than the money though, I wanted the sales team to be Safe Souls by supporting the person who had given us the opportunity in the first place. I hoped the pending launch would be infused with positivity, focus, and teamwork. I did not want anyone to feel ostracized for his sound business decisions. Maybe I'm a dreamer, but that will always be the standard I strive to create around me.

I'm not sure if everyone truly came around on the new pricing, but we did have a wildly-successful launch. And while some may not have enjoyed being gently called out on their less-than-stellar attitudes, I'm sure it gave them food for thought.

Let's all just aim to get along, support one another, and cover each other's backs.

YOU'RE FIRED!

I think my strong desire for everyone to feel the joy and freedom of having their backs covered by 'their people' stems from the fact that I have often felt the pain of it not occurring.

Time and time again, the same life lesson was repeated, but I just wasn't seeing that I was surrounding myself with unsafe souls and that I was addicted to their approval. The universe was trying to show me that I needed to be more discerning. But

I wasn't getting it. Can you relate to having to learn the same lessons over and over again?

In my last year at Capilano University, I took a required course called Cap Ads. It was a marketing and advertising course that spanned the entire year. My team of four colleagues and I had all worked diligently and had achieved an "A" on the first portion of the campaign in the fall semester. Our final presentation was due at the end of the following spring semester—about a month away. I was excited. We had created an innovative campaign for this mandatory course in our business school. Mediocrity was not an option.

Then it went south.

My teammates called a meeting at which they announced I was no longer part of the group. What? They cited that it was because I couldn't attend all the necessary work sessions. This was true—I was the only one in the group who worked close to full-time hours throughout college—but I was a Dean's List student and always performed. I was totally shocked by their news.

But in fine fashion, I sucked it up, numbed out my raw emotions, and went about finding another team who could use my talents. I did, and we excelled. It was a crazy month, but we got it done. Creativity and productivity flowed so widely and I now understand the difference—this new group was a sisterhood of Safe Souls. We were all free to do our parts without criticism, with support, and with personal integrity assumed among each member. There were no negative blocks. We had so much fun together and it showed up in how successful we were when delivering our campaign for that final and important grade.

I confess that the sting of rejection by my former team was still pretty sore, so I was secretly happy to hear that they had only achieved a "B" for their final presentation. Yes, there was still healing necessary! Had I truly been operating as a Safe Soul, I would have understood that their actions towards me were actually nothing to do with them; they were to do with me and my growth. They had provided me with a valuable lesson and today I'm grateful for it.

Years later, when I was in touch with myself enough to allow for unashamed vulnerability, I asked one of my former classmates why they just ousted me like that? She said, "Since we were in business school, we were emulating what a business would do. They would fire a perceived non-performer." Wow. In my experience managing many teams and serving on numerous boards, this is never the correct course of action—particularly in light of Safe Souls. First, I would call a review meeting and table any complaints. Then I would give an employee or teammate the opportunity to listen, communicate, and improve. He might even be able to shed light on any incorrect criticism being place on him unfairly.

But instead they blindsided me.

Recently, I ran into one of the guys in the group. He said he had always felt bad about how things had happened. He told me that a certain gal—I'll refrain from using names—had been the ringleader on the Cap Ads ousting. Not surprisingly, it was the same girl who had been the ringleader in the 'Sharpie on the locker' incident in high school. Some people just have to take others out to boost themselves up. Years later, I was able to totally forgive her after I learned a really interesting piece of information. Her actions were, in part, spawned by a survival tactic embedded in a woman's DNA—take out the perceived competition so that you will be the one that procreates.[4] This is a whole book in itself, so I'll leave it at that, but it is truly fascinating and worth some study. It helps me look upon some people's actions with love and compassion rather than with contempt and disbelief. We all just want to feel safe and secure and if someone doesn't have the tools to foster that, she may subconsciously default to her DNA.

I tell these stories because they have very similar threads. They involve people operating as what we call unsafe souls. I

4. www.understandmen.com/extreme_queen/

share them to highlight and contrast—unsafe vs. Safe Souls. Sometimes we need to see and feel the darkness to commit to operating in the light.

Everyone has the capacity to do the right thing, but some chose not to. Even when presented with the concepts of Safe Souls, some people continue to engage in GTC. It is this group we feel are unsafe souls. These individuals do not always have other's best interests at heart and can therefore be toxic. There comes a time when we each have to decide whether someone is a Safe Soul or an unsafe soul for us. If they are unsafe, with regret and love, we may have to let them go for our own wellbeing and for the wellbeing of those we care about.

IV. PRIVATE/PUBLIC PRAISE

Washington State Psychologist of the Year, author/co-author of *Ten Lessons to Transform Your Marriage*, *And Baby Makes Three*, and *The Marriage Clinic Casebook*, co-founder/President of The Gottman Institute, and co-creator of the immensely popular weekend workshop *Art and Science of Love*, Dr. Julie Schwartz Gottman is an expert on relationships. Her extensive studies regarding what factors keep couples happy and together long-term often come down to a few simple practices.

Anger management is one practice. "Kindness doesn't mean that we don't express our anger," she explains, "but kindness informs how we choose to express the anger. You can throw spears at your partner. Or you can explain why you're hurt and angry, and that's the kinder path."

The other practice is praise. Dr. Gottman asserts, "There's a habit of mind that the masters have which is this: they are scanning their social environment for things they can appreciate and say thank you for. They are building this culture of respect and appreciation very purposefully. Disasters are scanning the social environment for partners' mistakes."[5]

5. http://www.collective-evolution.com/2014/11/20/social-science-says-lasting-relationships-come-down-to-2-basic-traits/

I wholeheartedly agree. Praise makes us feel great. Whether it's done privately or publically, it helps us feel like we are seen, heard, and, most importantly, appreciated. We all crave what Alison Armstrong, author of *The Queen's Code* and founder of PAX Programs Inc., simply calls 'status.' We need to feel noticed. We want significance. We love it when our accomplishments or simply our being is acknowledged. And when others give us this gift of 'status,' it diffuses our need to compete. This causes peace among people and ushers in safety.

Praise is a powerful tool. Pick it up often because when we praise others, we give them a gift with many returns. The conscious decision to praise forces us to see another person for who they are and to acknowledge their many talents. Telling someone the positive things we experience about them can also push us out of our comfort zone—we are not very versed in voicing pure praise for someone. But so much positive knowledge is passed along through praise, it encourages personal growth, and it fosters the growth of our relationships with others, so we should strive do it often.

Let another praise you, and not your own mouth;
someone else, and not your own lips.

~ Proverbs 27:2

I love taking a friend's hand, looking her in the eye, and saying, "You are a rock star! How you handled yourself in that situation was amazing." Or, "You are such a goddess. What a fabulous retreat you just led. Do you know the impact you have had on all of these participants? I hope you really get that you are truly a genius at what you do."

These comments can go a long way in empowering people to step even more fully into their gifts and this makes the world a better place. Private praise is so easy to do.

Public praise is a blast too, and I love being its catalyst.

CORPORATE LOVE FEAST

While presenting a Safe Souls workshop to a group of twenty-four people, I told them that the last assignment of the day was going to be a writing exercise. "In your folders, there are some sheets of paper listing everybody's name with a few lines below each. Please write down three things you really appreciate about each person. Examples can be anything from the person having a really cool style, to what an effective leader she is at work, to what a great dad he is. It could be anything you really admire or appreciate in your colleague." I did not tell the group what they would be doing with the list.

They got busy writing.

There are a few reasons why I have participants physically write out their praises. Firstly, when you're writing by hand, a group of cells at the base of your brain, called the reticular activating system (RAS), are stimulated. The RAS acts as a filter, causing your brain to focus more intently on that which you are actively engaged. Author Henriette Anne Klauser says in her book, *Write It Down, Make It Happen*: "Writing triggers the RAS, which in turn sends a signal to the cerebral cortex, 'Wake up! Pay attention! Don't miss this detail!' Once you write down your goal [or your praise] your brain will be working overtime to see you get it."

Secondly, I believe writing can help us change any negative thoughts we may be harboring into more positive ones. It can ultimately become a powerful, spiritual practice. When your conscious mind, and even your subconscious mind, is engaged more deeply in what you're writing, you will also remember it more easily. It will start to become part of the fiber of your being. I think writing down praise items truly gets people into the mode of purposefully and habitually thinking positively.

Lastly, if you are asked to share your praises publically, your mind may short circuit. The faintest ink is better than the strongest memory.

Once all the pens were still, I said, "Next, we're going to go around the room and share what we've written, that is, if you are comfortable doing so."

I looked at the clock—it had taken them quite a while to write their praises down—and I wondered if we were going to have time to complete this whole exercise. There were a lot of people and each had about seventy-two praise items to share. So I gave them the option of either reading one item or all three things about each person. Everyone was sitting in a U-shape, so we started on my left. Bruce was the first man to receive the flurry of compliments from his teammates. One by one, they publicly praised him. I learned that he was incredibly loved, respected, and appreciated by all the detailed descriptives and praises they showered upon him. In the span of a few minutes, I got to know him better than I might have in a year. Then they went to Henry. One by one, they praised him, too. The genuine emotion circulating was palpable.

As we continued around the room, I was shocked at what occurred. Not only did they say all three items—in some occasions they went on to say other things. There were tears. There was laughter. There was love. The person receiving the public praise would often respond by sharing what they were feeling. Every word spoken was incredibly positive, loving, and generous. We went through about four people and I quickly did the math. It was taking eight minutes per person. So I simply declared, "Instead of finishing early as I anticipated prior to starting this exercise, we are going to use every minute of our six-hour time allotment."

John, who runs the organization, looked at me and said, "Oh yes, we're definitely finishing this!" We were literally three hours in that room praising each other. It was a blessing for everyone. Praising publicly lifted the whole vibration of the meeting, and ultimately the company. There was so much love. Participants understood their value, in some cases, for the first time. It freed people up to be themselves.

For example, one woman was praised by many of her co-workers as being incredibly detail-oriented and they loved this about her because it made her dependable. They knew that if they put a project in front of her, it would get done correctly. Her level of perfection was consistent. Later, when we were out socializing, she said, "Oh my gosh! I couldn't believe what I heard. I used to go into work thinking I was driving them all crazy. I'm so detailed, I figured I was a nightmare to them."

She was operating in a low vibration and insecure place and the public praise from her colleagues elevated her. It also brought the whole team together because when you start seeing somebody through the positive eyes of another, it can change your view of that person as well. That's the ripple effect when we praise people publicly—others can see them through a different lens and that lens can be a magnifying glass for good.

I love the feeling I get when I hear somebody being praised. Unfortunately, it doesn't happen that often. In our world, for some reason, we're not very generous with praising people in public. This is something I'd love to facilitate and witness as a major movement on the planet. It will shift when people start seeing its value. Praise raises people up to new places and that eventually benefits everybody.

I recently read an account of how an African tribe handles a person who has done something wrong. They take the culprit to the center of the village and the tribe surrounds him for two days. They spend that time praising him for all the good he has done in the past—they praise him publicly. The tribe believes that each person is inherently good, but sometimes they make mistakes. They believe that these mistakes are really a cry for help. By praising him rather than punishing him, they unite in order to reconnect him with his good nature.

If this is true, it's amazing. If not, it's a concept and practice we should modify and adopt so it can work in our culture. We may not be able to gather for two days, but we sure can make a concerted effort to come together and edify the person with our words of affirmation.

CHANGE IS POSSIBLE

It seems like a daunting task—influencing a planet full of souls to treat each other kindly. But I believe it is possible. One or two at a time. Then one or two hundred at a time. Then one or two thousand at a time. My vision is that millions then billions of people adopt a Safe Souls lifestyle. This really would bring peace and prosperity to the planet. People would be free to explore their individuality without the fear of being taken out by their tribe because of it. People would look for ways to praise their brother or sister, rather than looking for ways to lambaste them. People would have more direct communication rather than the multitude of side conversations occurring today that really don't solve anything. Life as we know it would be different...better.

KRISTEAN GETS IT

When I met my husband and his sons, they unknowingly communicated in deep levels of gossip, triangulation, and criticism. It was how they grew up and they just thought it was normal. Guys get together and talk about each other, right? It was common and expected.

When I told them that I was not comfortable with it, they thought I was just being a hypersensitive woman. I don't think they considered how amazing relationships could be if each person operated at the highest level of integrity. They did not see that gossip, triangulation, and criticism were hurting their relationships with one another, with their friends, and with their colleagues. This was not entirely their fault—it was simply a way of operating that they had learned through osmosis. But things can change.

Recently, I heard my youngest 'bonus' son, Kristean, having a conversation with his dad. "How is your brother doing?"

Ken asked. (Ken was inquiring about a son he had not been in relationship with for quite some time, due to unresolved and unsafe soul situations.)

"You know, that's not a conversation I'm going to engage in, because we're talking about my brother and he isn't here. I just don't want to get into that conversation. I'd be triangulating." Boom. He got it. Prior to understanding the distinction, he likely would have gone into a long discourse about how his brother was doing this, that, and the other, and it wouldn't necessarily have been favorable.

While not everyone understands the value of this level of communication, Safe Souls has improved most of our relationships significantly—and it has helped us build much deeper friendships.

Implementing Safe Souls is like flexing a muscle—it's a dumbbell we work out with and teach others to lift as well. It's a whole new way of relating for most people. The message is to simply stop engaging in gossip, triangulation, and criticism. If these creep into the conversation, we quickly course-correct and move onto different topics. The beauty of this is that it has taught us more about where we are now and where we are going, than gossiping ever did. We now talk more about interesting ideas, our dreams, and the future, rather than about people, their personal affairs, and the past.

Practicing Safe Souls is like being on a diet. When you get rid of the bad—the sugars, processed foods, and unhealthy fats— you have to replace these calorie vacancies with something else. Now you have room for healthy fats, muscle-building proteins, and energy-producing complex carbohydrates, like greens. So when we get together as Safe Souls, we're really replacing the time that might have been spent unconsciously talking about others, with new, healthy, and empowering conversations. We get to share enlightening things and we leave the garbage out.

Fillers (GTC), like simple carbohydrates, are replaced with something far better for us, which is speaking about a much more powerful future—our goals, our dreams, and how we can support each other. Safe Souls ends up enriching our level of conversation.

Exercise #5: Active Healing

Think deeply—are there unresolved issues at home, at work, or within your friendships that need addressing? Do you have unsafe situations for which you need to apologize? Do you feel the nudge to reconnect with someone who has hurt you? You can be the catalyst for healing. Write down your thoughts and commit to taking action.

_____

_____

_____

_____

_____

_____

_____

_____

_____

_____

_____

_____

_____

_____

CHAPTER 7

IMPLEMENTATION

*Organizations are successful because of good
implementation, not good business plans.*

~ Guy Kawasaki

THE PROCESS WITHIN AN ORGANIZATION

There are many ways to implement Safe Souls within companies,
schools, families, and even within a group of friends.

To teach Safe Souls within a company, we have developed a
workshop and love presenting it to organizations both large and
small. You can also affect change in your workplace by reading
this book and using the process described herein. But perhaps the
most effective way of causing change is a combination of both.
Using an outside trainer to present the distinctions company-wide
and then having leaders within the organization monitor progress
and coach the Safe Souls way of operating post-workshop, is ideal.

One part of the formula—using an outside trainer—is incredibly
useful as people often feel more comfortable talking to someone
neutral about work-related issues and interpersonal challenges.
If an employee talks to his boss or a colleague about sensitive
subjects, he will likely edit himself instinctively.

Another advantage of having a formal Safe Souls workshop
within an organization is that the pre-workshop protocol of
interviewing the leadership and a few key personnel is very
enlightening. Becoming aware of the issues and pitfalls within
an organization is helpful for tailoring the discussion to things

117

relevant to that particular group of people. An outsider can become very valuable, as team members won't always open up to someone within their tribe. And even if they did, they might not be skilled in dealing with the emotional fallout of sharing things that may have been suppressed for years.

Finally, the company's administration might be biased. They might not want to address certain subjects, as they themselves may be involved in some of the pertinent issues. Sometimes they cannot step far enough away to see the problems or take responsibility for their own actions. Someone from outside a company can present a fresh, unbiased perspective of the real issues and can be honest and forthright without any agenda or fear of consequences. They can call it as they see it.

Reading and distributing this book is still an essential part of the process, even if you decide to have a Safe Souls trainer provide services for your company, because you and your team can be prepared and expectant. You can start flexing your own Safe Souls muscle, making the changes easier and more expedient for everyone.

ASSESSMENT

When we first engage a company, we spend time getting the lay of the land—we meet the administration, describe the process, talk about expectations, and get any background that might be helpful. We encourage questions and provide some essential ground rules. One of the most important is our role: we are there to help companies become healthier, more harmonious, and, ultimately, more profitable.

While we do interview team members pre-workshop and encourage openness, we are not all therapists or counselors. And while it is very helpful to know the emotional climate of a company before beginning a workshop, we try to avoid having team members tell us personal details about specific people. We personify Safe Souls from the outset. However, on a few occasions, team members have revealed very private and specific information about another person, so we begin teaching Safe Souls right then and there.

This brings up the question of confidentiality. Everything within a Safe Souls pre-workshop interview, during the workshop itself, and the post-workshop follow-up, is held in the strictest confidence. This is the only way to foster Safe Souls and to cause change within an organization.

Now, be aware that gossip can sometimes come disguised as 'confidentiality.' How many times, in the normal course of conversations, have you heard the words, "You have to promise not to tell anyone...x, y, or z." This is not confidentiality. It's a red flag. Anything following those words will likely violate the No GTC rule. If you agree to keeping a secret, you are probably engaging in gossip, likely triangulating, and often will be listening to criticism. None create Safe Souls. The human part of you, the part that adores knowing juicy details, would love to allow the speaker to continue, but the spirit-driven Safe Soul in you will ask him to refrain.

Usually, you cannot be a keeper of secrets and a Safe Souls practitioner simultaneously. Generally, they are mutually exclusive. It's a discipline, but well worth it. It keeps discussions kind, clean, and clear. It frees up your mind from having to remember who said what, what you're allowed to repeat or not, and also protects you from any toxicity that the 'secret sharer' would have imparted. Refraining from listening is also the perfect opportunity to share Safe Souls with the speaker. Most are simply unaware of the effects of their words.

In the course of a private pre-workshop interview, we do encourage openness, but only for the sake of the greater good. This is different from secret telling for the sake of sharing or acquiring juicy details for no reason. If we are asked to keep something to ourselves in a workshop environment, we will hold that confidence and help the person work through her issue. We will assist her in finding solutions and formulating possibilities of how she might eventually talk to the other party. This is another example of a Committed Conversation for Action.

CONFIDENTIAL PRE-WORKSHOP SURVEY

Prior to a Safe Souls workshop, we forward surveys to the team members and administration. We ask that they be filled out anonymously, unless they prefer otherwise, and be sent back within a month of the scheduled workshop. This assessment tool gives us a sense of the corporate culture and provides helpful insights regarding patterns and consistencies. We are often astounded by the toxicity of an organization, but frankly, this gets us even more excited to teach them a better way—a Safe Souls way.

In the survey, we ask questions such as:

- How do you feel about going to work—do you feel supported? Understood? Included? Empowered?

- Are there any interpersonal issues hindering your happiness and productivity at work? (We ask them to omit specific names.)

- Do you ever spend time socially with your teammates? Or are they strictly business relationships?

- Do you see this as a long-term place of employment? If yes, why? If not, why? (We remind them that this is strictly confidential.)

- What is the communication style at your place of work?

- Is there anything else you can tell us about your company's culture that might help us create the most impactful workshop? Our mission is to help foster more positive, productive, and powerful relationships in the workplace and beyond. You can help by providing any information you think pertinent.

INTERVIEWING KEY PERSONNEL

Identifying one or more key people to share more deeply about the corporate ethos can be very helpful. It can give us an honest and broad picture of the company's interpersonal issues and concerns that may not have come out in the written survey. We do this following the protocols mentioned earlier. This is not meant to be gossipy or to target individuals, but rather to discover areas in which the entire organization can improve. We choose the language and questions carefully to elicit broad answers, rather than specifics about certain people. If they wish to explain a particular situation, we will ask the person being interviewed to refrain from using names, as they are not ultimately necessary.

PRE-WORKSHOP SESSION

Once we have gathered the data, we create a report and share it with the organization's leader. This report provides feedback on specific areas in which the company is flourishing and also highlights areas in which it could use some assistance. We also reference this information when deciding which areas to emphasize during the workshop.

At this time, usually within a few weeks of the workshop, we offer specific feedback and suggestions to the key personnel to help start the process of change. They can begin flexing the Safe Souls muscle before the workshop even begins. This invariably expedites transformation—both during and post-workshop.

WORKSHOPS

Depending on the size of the group, a full Safe Souls workshop will run anywhere from four to six hours. This includes presenting the distinction, group discussions, writing exercises, paired sharing, one-on-one sharing, and a question-and-answer period. We also condense the material to a shorter format—one to two hours—if time is limited.

OBSERVATION

Another way of performing an assessment is to be a proverbial fly on the wall. During a workshop, we will listen intently and take in as much information as possible about a company's ethos. Even during breaks, we look for patterns. Are people whispering, excluding anyone, or is there a ringleader influencing others—for good or for bad? What are the non-verbal clues saying? At this point, we do not intervene, we just observe and subtly take notes for the purpose of edification. We can gather valuable information this way, which we compile for later in the workshop or in a post-workshop follow-up session. Simply observing can be very helpful.

In one workshop I noticed a woman who was very popular and clearly a leader, but who also seemed somewhat insecure. My sense was that jealousy existed toward her from some of the ladies in the group. She was showing the classic 'feeling unsafe' symptoms—she seemed to stay in her shell, seemed to be in fight-or-flight mode, and seemed to want to shrink rather than shine. All this was very subtle. On the surface, you would have seen an outgoing, fun-loving person.

I spoke with her during a break and asked her if my observations were accurate. Thankfully she was an opening for truth and shared that, yes, it was accurate. "I often feel like I should fly under the radar for fear of being judged for my commitment to excellence. I think that if I lead too strongly, or at all, my peers will take me out. I will be perceived as a threat, not a teammate, when really I'm just trying to use my skills to further us all."

How sad for her, for her company, and even for her colleagues. Here was a woman with infinite skills and abilities, but who was afraid to shine for fear of annihilation.

I was able to strategically incorporate this valuable information into the balance of the workshop. I shared about the devastating effects of envy and jealously and how it wreaks havoc on a soul and often causes the subject to feel bullied and ultimately to want to fade into the background. I reminded them that a rising tide lifts all boats—we should want our colleagues to be successful! We should want to encourage them to excel. We should want them to feel free to bring their best game to the field. Just being a kind person is not enough though; encourage your teammates because their success is good for your life, too. Better ideas will be generated, better communication will ensue, and bottom lines will be increased. This benefits everyone. So avoid being a catalyst for shrinkage by being jealous or envious of another's successful traits. Instead be a catalyst for expansion by celebrating your fellow man (and woman).

After speaking this truth to the group, I could feel the energy shift in the woman with whom I had spoken during the break. It was like an invisible cloud lifted from her. She began to participate more freely. Since she was a popular and engaging woman already, the change may not have been noticeable to some, but I was clear on the shift. So was she. She was no longer guarded; she was free to be herself.

POST-WORKSHOP

After a workshop, we follow up periodically to see how Safe Souls is working within an organization and to provide any needed support. Depending on the agreement with the company, we might also follow up with each employee to provide them with individual support, and to receive feedback. We may even return to the company for a post-workshop session with the whole group or for a follow-up workshop with new employees.

One of the tools with which we provide workshop participants is the Safe Souls Zone sign. We borrowed the idea from a company who, after hearing about the Safe Souls way of operating, decided to create their own reminders. They printed the *No Gossip + No Triangulation + No Criticism = Safe Souls* formula and posted one at each workstation. What a great reminder! So we created an official Safe Souls Zone sign—including the basic No GTC formula *and* the Fourth and Fifth Dimensions—and started including it in the workshop packages. Thank you Piranha Marketing for the great idea!

transforming relationships
through the power of kindness

SAFE SOULS ZONE

NO GTC!

- No Gossiping about others negatively
- No Triangulating, i.e., bringing your grievance to a third party rather than directly to the person
- No Criticizing others' opinions, appearances, religious beliefs, behaviors, philosophies, or political affiliations (or any other personal preferences)

FOURTH DIMENSION

- Practice Safe Souls not only in your speaking, practice it in your *thinking*.

FIFTH DIMENSION

- No gossiping about, triangulating with, or criticizing *ourselves*!

ORGANIC TRANSFORMATION

The Safe Souls distinction is simple and static, but its implementation in companies is diverse and dynamic. It is organic and grows over time. We plant the seeds during a workshop, but then it is up to the company and individuals to water them. This watering causes Safe Souls to flourish within the organization and ultimately beyond its borders into the community.

Paul Mitchell Salon Schools created an annual program in which they give out free hugs to anyone willing to receive them. They head to the streets, hold up colorful "Free Hugs" signs, and provide something positive to their community. There are over one hundred Paul Mitchell Schools nationwide and every school is connected on Free Hugs Day. I have not been directly involved in a Free Hugs Day, but apparently the community impact is amazing. It is our sincere hope and mission to have Safe Souls make its way into schools, families, and communities in the same organic way that free hugs have found their way onto the streets.

As Paul Mitchell's students have embraced Free Hugs Day, imagine if students everywhere adopted No GTC. Bullying would virtually be eradicated, as all bullying begins with criticism. It usually involves gossip and most definitely uses triangulation as a tactic as well. Safe Souls would not only protect the victims of bullying, it could also turn the would-be-bullies into kinder, more empathetic members of their communities. This would be a dream come true, a mission accomplished. Teaching kids this distinction early on would not only transform the schoolyard, it would ultimately revolutionize boardroom dynamics. As young students become adults and enter into the workforce, they would already be operating as Safe Souls.

CHAPTER 8

WE ARE ONE

*If we have no peace, it is because we have
forgotten that we belong to each other.*

~ Mother Teresa

Safe Souls is for all souls as it can positively impact each individual on the planet. It embraces every race, religion, and culture, without asking anyone to forgo or alter his or her core religious, spiritual, or philosophical beliefs. Everyone has the potential to fulfill a more powerful destiny by implementing the simple tenets of the Safe Souls distinction.

As part of the human experience, we feel naturally compelled to focus on the differences between what our faith teaches and what another's faith teaches. We likely do this because we need to know that our beliefs are the 'right' beliefs, that our religion is the 'truth,' that our guru was the one and only 'enlightened' leader. We want the comfort of knowing that our 'path' is an accurate way to this concept called heaven. Or we want to know that our next 'incarnation' will be more enlightened due to our living an honorable life this time around. We especially do not want to be 'lost' by following the wrong way! But let's put these differences and concerns aside for a moment and concentrate on the similarities.

Religious, spiritual, and philosophical lines are often blurred, as there are so many parallels among the various belief systems. Most offer the same basic message: "Honor your own soul, as well as your neighbor's, to truly serve the faith or teacher you follow." This may be a controversial statement, as a few religions are thought of as radical, even evil. However, I try to remember the elementary recommendation to "never judge a man until you have walked a mile in his shoes." If you were raised in a certain part of the world and were offered the teachings of a specific faith, you would inevitably wind up with very strong convictions around that belief system. So who are you to judge another's convictions, just because they are different than yours? Of course, we can pull some pretty crazy verses out of the Bible, the Qu'ran, and the Torah, that speak of murdering non-believers, and could say, "See, those Christians, Muslims, and Jewish people are bad." But I think we should turn around and look at ourselves before pointing the finger at anyone else. We have not walked in anyone's shoes except our own and we certainly can't pretend to be expert interpreters of these ancient scriptures or to know with certainty that they are even inspired texts. Safe Souls is our responsibility in spite of what anyone else believes. We can be the change we want to see in the world. The sooner we do this, the sooner we will have peace in our own hearts, and the sooner we will see peace on earth.

Regardless of your religion or how you live your life in this often-volatile world, when you practice Safe Souls, you are committing to being good to yourself and to everyone around you. There are no exceptions. And this is nothing new—it is right in line with most of the teachings from the eight largest religions in the world, which warn us about our speech and about that which resides in our hearts. Most religions tell us to keep our words and our hearts pure. I'll touch on some verses as taught through the eight most prevalent faiths.[6] In order of their global reach, these groups are:

Christianity: 2,200,000,000 followers

Islam: 1,600,000,000 followers

Hinduism: 1,100,000,000 followers

Buddhism: 488,000,000 followers

Taoism: 12 - 173,000,000 followers

Shinto: 100,000,000 followers

6. https://en.wikipedia.org/wiki/Major_religious_groups

Sikhism: 28,000,000 followers

Judaism: 14,000,000 followers

While these religions may seem worlds apart, they have commonalities noticeable in their written texts—the Bible, the Qur'an, the Bhagavad Gita, the Torah, etc. The wise King Solomon was likely right thousands of years ago when he wrote, "There is nothing new under the sun." Perhaps there are simply different ways each faith expresses similar goals, most of which are in alignment with Safe Souls. If we all adhered to the common and honorable teachings, it would be magical.

I will share with you the Universal Rules, followed by some significant messages contained in the most widespread sacred texts. I find they are a wonderful source of inspiration—a testament to how we might strive to live so we can make a positive impact on the lives of those around us. Perhaps you will agree.

THE TWO UNIVERSAL RULES: GOLDEN AND SILVER

The Golden Rule can be found in some form in almost every ethical and religious tradition. It states that you should treat others as you would like to be treated.

The Silver Rule is the cautionary form of the Golden Rule and states that you should not treat others in a way that you would not like to be treated.

Using these two rules alone, we can create Safe Souls in our worlds! Imagine what that would lead to? It could create a shelter—a virtual haven—for everyone with whom we come in contact. The world can be stormy, but we can create peace within our own surroundings. We can be the Butterfly Effect. We have power over, and responsibility for, our speech and our listening. Being a Safe Soul in both is totally doable and will inevitably inspire others to follow suit.

People have said to me, "Oh, no. You haven't seen my workplace. Safe Souls would be impossible to implement." Or, "You don't understand my family—it's a toxic mess."

Actually I do. I've been in seemingly impossible and totally toxic situations, too. Everybody faces them at one point or the other and Safe Souls really can be transformative. It can create a shelter from the storm; it can even calm the storm entirely. If you have even the smallest bit of hope that operating in this new way might change things in your life and in the lives of those around you, have the courage to give it a try. The Golden and Silver Rules are great examples of operating as a Safe Soul. The various and predominant world religions and philosophies all contain similar teachings. We will explore these next.

CHRISTIANITY

In Christianity, the Bible has a lot to say about love, kindness, gossiping, and judging. A few passages that speak to these notions are:

A man who is kind benefits himself,
but a cruel man hurts himself.

~ Proverbs 11:17

Above all these put on love, which binds everything
together in perfect harmony.

~ Colossians 3:14

A gossip betrays a confidence, but a
trustworthy man keeps a secret.

~ Proverbs 11:13

Besides, they get into the habit of being idle and going
about from house to house. And not only do they become
idlers, but also gossips and busybodies, saying things
that they ought not to.

~ 1 Timothy 5:13

Do not judge, or you too will be judged.

~ Matthew 7:1

At the time the Bible was written, the concept of triangulation may not have been formalized, but if it had been, my guess is that much would have been said about avoiding it also.

ISLAM

Those who act kindly in this world will have kindness.

~ Qur'an 39.10

You who believe, if some perverse man should come up to you with some piece of news, clear up the facts lest you afflict some folk out of ignorance and some morning feel regretful for what you may have done.

~ Qur'an 49.6

Treat people in such a way and live amongst them in such a manner that if you die they will weep over you; alive they crave for your company.

~ Nahjul Balagha, Saying 9

Given the recent rise of geopolitical and religious-based world upset and terrorism, I hesitated to even speak about the Qur'an as it has been the source of much debate and division. It has become very easy to paint the entire population of Muslims with an "evil" brush, without understanding that the radicals do not represent the faith as a whole. Cleary, throughout history, there have been radicals in many religious denominations who have committed heinous acts in the name of their faith—have started wars, have engaged in terrorism, have murdered, have harbored hatred, have not honored themselves or their neighbor—but let's not fall into the trap of repaying hate with hate or painting an entire people group with a brush that should be reserved for a select few. Even a quick Google search of "what verses in the Bible (or the Torah) advocate killing non-believers?" will provide you with much food for thought. Safe Souls aims to "love another as you love yourself," regardless of each other's religious beliefs or moral philosophies. I believe this is the right thing to do. If someone is caught in the chains of hatred and evil, your love could very well be the antidote.

BUDDHISM

Speak not harshly to anyone. Those thus addressed
will retort. Painful, indeed, is vindictive speech.
Blows in exchange may bruise you.

~ Dhammapada 133

The essence of all religion is love, compassion and tolerance.
Kindness is my true religion. No matter whether you
are learned or not, whether you believe in the next life
or not, whether you believe in God or Buddha or some other
religion or not, in day-to-day life you must be a kind person.
When you are motivated by kindness, it doesn't matter
whether you are a practitioner, a lawyer, a politician, an
administrator, a worker, or an engineer—whatever your
profession or field, deep down you are a kind person.
Love, compassion and tolerance are necessities, not luxuries.
Without them, humanity cannot survive.

~ His Holiness the Dalai Lama

When we feel love and kindness toward others, it not only
makes others feel loved and cared for, but it helps us also
develop inner happiness and peace.

~ The 14th Dalai Lama (1935)

Tenderness and kindness are not the signs of weakness
and despair, but of strength and resolution.

~ Kahlil Gibran (1883-1931)

In Buddhism, loving-kindness is a meditation practice, which brings about a sweetening of old, habituated, negative patterns of the mind. First, you must develop a loving self-acceptance. Then, Buddhism teaches that you must systematically develop loving-kindness toward others—first toward a respected person such as a spiritual teacher, then toward a dearly beloved such as a close family member or friend, and then toward a neutral person such as someone you know, but don't have any special feelings toward. Lastly, you must develop loving-kindness toward a hostile person such as someone with whom you are currently having difficulty. Send loving-kindness toward yourself and the groups above in that order.

How do we develop these feelings? We can do this by:

- **Visualizing**: imagining you and him smiling at each other and being joyous
- **Reflecting**: thinking about her positive qualities and the kind things she has done
- **Saying**: repeating a mantra such as 'loving-kindness' while thinking about him

True loving kindness, brought about in this manner, will create beautifully Safe Souls.

HINDUISM

Lord Krishna, the possessor of all opulences said:
Fearlessness, pure heartedness, established in the wisdom of discrimination of spirit and matter by the science of uniting the individual consciousness with the Ultimate Consciousness, charity,
self-restraint, performance of sacrifice, study of Vedic scriptures, austerity, uprightness, nonviolence, truthfulness, aversion to fault finding, compassion to all being, absence of

*avarice, gentleness, modesty and determination. O Arjuna,
radiance, forgiveness, fortitude, purity, freedom from malice,
absence of pride arise in one born of the divine nature.*

~ Bhagavad Gita Chapter 16 Verses 1-3

*One giving false evidence or uttering
falsehood goes to Raurava hell.*

~ Markandeya Puranao

*Condemn none: if you can stretch out a
helping hand, do so. If you cannot, fold your hands,
bless your brothers, and let them go their own way.*

~ Swami Vivekananda

Practiced primarily in India and Nepal, Hinduism is the
world's third largest religion. It is said to be the oldest religion
and prescribes eternal duties such as honesty, refraining from
injuring living beings, patience, forbearance, self-restraint, and
compassion.[7] After spending time in Kathmandu and trekking
through the Khumbu Valley en route to Mount Everest base camp,
I was amazed at the kindness and gentleness of the Nepalese
people. Nepal is 81.3% Hindu and 9% Buddhist, so given the
Hindu "duties" along with the Buddhist philosophy, it's not
surprising that this country's people were lovely. I could hardly
speak with most of those I met, but still felt like I was surrounded
by Safe Souls.

TAOISM

*In Taoism when you gossip, you break all the rules
of compassion and wisdom. It is the inflation of ego
and blocks a person's path.*

~ Chuang Tzu 3-1

---

7. https://en.wikipedia.org/wiki/Hinduism

Kindness in words creates confidence. Kindness in thinking creates profoundness. Kindness in giving creates love.

~ Lao Tzu

Taoism is of Chinese origin and emphasizes living in harmony with the Tao, a concept signifying "way," "path," "route," or sometimes more loosely, "doctrine" or "principle." Taoist propriety and ethics may vary depending on the particular school, but in general they tend to emphasize wu-wei (action through non-action), "naturalness," simplicity, spontaneity, and the Three Treasures: compassion, moderation, and humility.[8] I find that compassion and humility in particular dovetail perfectly with Safe Souls. When we are compassionate, we walk in love rather than fear. When we are humble, we have very little room for GTC. Even a few hours spent studying the foundational text of Taoism, the Tao Te Ching, will leave you with a sense that those who really follow Taoism are automatically living as Safe Souls.

SHINTO

Shinto is essentially a religion of gratitude and love.

~ W.G. Aston, *Shinto, the Way of the Gods*

One could say that being a Shintoist consists in feeling that one is a member of the Japanese community. Only very rarely are philosophic or religious movements so clearly and exclusively tied to a people to the degree that Shintoism is.

~ Michael Malherbe, *Les Religions de l'Humanité*

While there is no one core sacred text in Shinto for followers to study and espouse, it is still the largest religion in Japan, practiced by nearly 80% of the population. It is an action-centered religion focused on ritual practices to be carried out diligently. These rituals are meant to establish a connection between present-day Japan and its ancient past. Books of lore and historical accounts

8. https://en.wikipedia.org/wiki/Taoism

135

provide background and structure to many Shinto beliefs.

One tenet of Shinto, *kannagara,* refers to the law of natural order. Those who understand and adhere to *kannagara* know the divine, the human, and how people should live. From this knowledge stems the ethical dimension of Shinto, focusing on sincerity (*makoto*), honesty (*tadashii*) and purity.[9] These three domains complement Safe Souls beautifully.

SIKHISM

Your mouth has not stopped slandering and gossiping about others. Your service is useless and fruitless. Cruelty has not left your mind; you have not cherished kindness for other living beings.

~ Part of 1 Shabad from Parmananda,
Sri Guru Granth Sahib, p. 1253

Whosoever is kind to others, the Lord receives him with kindness.

~ Guru V, Gauri Rag

Be kind to all beings, this is more meritorious than bathing at the sixty-eight sacred shrines of pilgrimage and donating money.

~ Guru Granth Sahib Ji, 136

Sikhism, which means "one who seeks after truth" was founded by Guru Nanuk in the Punjab region of India during the 15th century. Followers believe there is one true God who should be worshiped wholeheartedly. One of the laws of Sikhism forbids gossiping, negative language, and worthless talk. We can see from the passages above that each Guru is teaching followers to walk in the spirit of kindness as prescribed by Safe Souls.

---

9. https://en.wikipedia.org/wiki/Shinto

JUDAISM

*Thou shalt not go up and down as
a tale-bearer among thy people.*

~ Leviticus 19:16

*Lashon ha-ra (disparaging speech) kills three:
the person who speaks it, the person who hears it,
and the person about whom it is told.*

~ Talmud, Arachin 15b

*The world stands upon three things: upon the Law,
upon worship, and upon showing kindness.*

~ Mishnah, Abot 1.2

Within the Jewish religion, speech and words are taken very seriously and the law forbids tale bearing, or gossip. Further, the Jewish tradition does not allow you to speak about another person, even if what is spoken is true, is not negative, is not secret, hurts no one, or even if the person himself would tell the same thing if asked.

Judaism asserts that gossip can even lead to bloodshed. The story of Doeg the Edomite, in the Torah's I Samuel 21 and 22, illustrates this belief. In the historical account, Doeg saw Ahimelech the Kohein give David bread and a sword, a completely innocent act intended to aid a leading member of Saul's court. Doeg reported this to Saul, but did not clearly communicate that Ahimelech was being helpful to David and thus, ultimately loyal to Saul. What Doeg shared seemed innocent—it was true, not negative, nor a secret. But Saul misinterpreted this tale as proof that Ahimelech was supporting David in a rebellion, and proceeded to slaughter Ahimelech and all but one of the Kohanim at Nob. Had Doeg refrained from gossip, many lives would have been spared. Gossip aside, in Judaism, every personal detail that one shares with another is automatically considered private, unless the person says otherwise.

Lashon ha-ra—literally, the 'evil tongue'—is the worst of the sins because it involves discrediting a person or saying negative things about a person, even if those negative things are true. Saying negative things that are *not* true—*motzisheimra*—and spreading these bad reports, is considered the worst offense. Clearly, Judaism supports the tenets offered in Safe Souls.

GROSS NATIONAL HAPPINESS

Bhutan, a small country at the eastern end of the Himalayas, brings national awareness to the quality of individuals' lives in an interesting and unusual way. They do not simply use the conventional measurements of a country's prosperity, such as Gross National Product (GNP), employment rates, or crime statistics; they assess their country's success in terms of its population's Gross National Happiness (GNH). The Fourth King of Bhutan, His Majesty Jigme Singye Wangchuck, coined the term in the early 1970s.

This philosophy is centered on taking a more holistic approach to measuring the country's sustainable progress by giving equal importance to the non-economic indicators of wellbeing as it does to the more conventional economic aspects. Bhutan has now become a real-life Shangri-La of sorts—since opening its borders to visitors about 40 years ago, people have flocked to the only country on earth to measure progress in this way.

In measuring GNH, four main pillars are evaluated:

- Sustainable socio-economic development
- Preservation and promotion of cultural values
- Conservation of the natural environment
- Establishment of good governance

By gauging these things collectively, officials measure their citizen's wellbeing. It is more all-encompassing, taking into account individuals seeking fulfillment as well as their contribution to the country. This creates awareness around improving the quality of people's lives and, therefore, their overall happiness. Does the country have a long way to go in terms of its general progress? By some measures, yes. However, it has advanced in many ways during the short time that GNH has been active.

Implementing Safe Souls within your organization, your family, and your group of friends, will have a similarly positive effect. Be patient though, as you may not see it immediately. In fact, Safe Souls can be a disruptive technology, so some relationships *may* get worse before they get better. Some people need time to adapt to No GTC and the Fourth and Fifth Dimensions, but if you persevere and stand for what is honorable, you and your circle will reap the rewards. Just as GNH may have seemed an insignificant or even worthless hypothesis at first, its benefits to the people of Bhutan have become far-reaching. Safe Souls can have this effect too.

MODERN DAY PHILOSOPHICAL LEADERS

People on a trajectory of spiritual growth seek out those they feel are enlightening. Whether we are looking to create change in a certain area of life or whether we are seeking an overall shift to be better connected, more purposeful, or more at peace, the wisdom from others can be invaluable. Deepak Chopra, Marianne Williamson, Robin Sharma, and the late Wayne Dyer are four examples of modern day philosophers that have been instrumental in my life. Each of them draws on the foundations from ancient religious texts and philosophers long passed and blends that with their own wisdom and enlightenment, creating a powerful combination for our modern and fast-paced world. Their wisdom fits beautifully with the Safe Souls way of life.

Two quotes by Deepak Chopra I find applicable are:

If you and I are having a single thought of violence or hatred against anyone in the world at this moment, we are contributing to the wounding of the world.

The secret of attraction is to love yourself. Attractive people judge neither themselves nor others. They are open to gestures of love. They think about love, and express their love in every action. They know that love is not a mere sentiment, but the ultimate truth at the heart of the universe.

Marianne Williamson reminds us to be Safe Souls through the following thoughts:

We are not held back by the love we didn't receive in the past, but by the love we're not extending in the present.

You may believe that you are responsible for what you do, but not for what you think. The truth is that you are responsible for what you think, because it is only at this level that you can exercise choice. What you do comes from what you think.

Quotes from Robin Sharma that pertain to No GTC and the Fourth and Fifth Dimensions are:

The price of greatness is responsibility over each of our thoughts.

People want to know that you are real. That you are decent, kind and trustworthy. They want to feel you and sense you and look into your eyes to see what you are made of. They want to know your passion for whatever it is you stand for. And when they sense that you are the real deal, they will open up to you. When they see that you have their best interests in mind, they will trust you—and keep your best interests in mind. Once they get that you are good, they'll be good to you. And your career (along with your life) will get to a place called 'world class' based on those trust connections.

Wayne Dyer spoke of Safe Souls in his messages:

When you judge another, you do not define them, you define yourself.

Your reputation is in the hands of others. That's what the reputation is. You can't control that. The only thing you can control is your character.

It seems to me that, whether it's through ancient texts and philosophers, or through current wisdom from thought leaders on a profoundly spiritual path, the message of Safe Souls is rampant. It may not have been put into such a distinct formula as No GTC plus the Fourth and Fifth Dimensions, but many leaders I admire and seek to emulate have taught its essence.

CHAPTER 9

ACHIEVING SAFE SOULS PERSONALLY

*The smallest act of kindness is worth more than
the greatest of intentions.*

~ Oscar Wilde

THE FOURTH DIMENSION

It dawned on me a few months ago, that during the span of a few days—and, yes, it did coordinate perfectly with my lunar cycle—Ken could do nothing right. He was irritating me at every turn. His words were jarring, his motions were annoying, and I didn't want to be in his presence. I became emotionally aloof and physically distant. This is totally abnormal in our relationship, so I'm sure he was completely confused.

Then it dawned on me that I was being an unsafe soul. I have always had a strong commitment to practicing Safe Souls in my *speaking*, but I also make every attempt to practice Safe Souls in my *thinking*. I realized in that moment though, the one person who deserved my heart the most was not receiving my best. My thoughts were toxic. My mind was full of criticism and personal judgment towards Ken and it was showing up in my words and actions, or lack thereof. The Fourth Dimension is really being mindful of practicing Safe Souls even in our thoughts.

> *Watch your thoughts, they become words;*
> *watch your words, they become actions;*
> *watch your actions, they become habits;*

watch your habits, they become character;
watch your character, for it becomes your destiny.

This famous quote has been attributed to many different people—Ralph Waldo Emerson, Chinese philosopher Lao Tzu, supermarket magnate Frank Outlaw, spiritual teacher Gautama Buddha, and the father of Margaret Thatcher. Regardless of its origins, it's powerful. If our thoughts can ultimately become our destiny, why not keep them kind, safe, and empowering? When I noticed I was being an unsafe soul towards Ken that lunar cycle day, I pulled out a few tools.

Firstly, I washed my mouth out with **SOAP**: I...Stopped... **O**wned it...**A**pologized...and **P**raised. Then I had a Clearing Conversation.

"Ken, I have to confess that I've been an unsafe soul in my thinking towards you."

Shocking, but this was no news to him!

"I've been harboring a lot of critical thoughts and I'm sorry. I'm not sure what's going on with me, but I love you and am committed to us having an amazing, fun, loving marriage. Who I have been the last few days is not in alignment with that. Please forgive me." He graciously did and we had a good laugh about what a Holstein cow I had been.

I don't beat myself up about occasional lapses into stinkin' thinkin.' In fact, if we were to say that our fellow man had never irritated us or we had never harbored unsafe thoughts, I believe we would be lying. The transformation is in how quickly, once we notice the deviation from our commitment, we course-correct. How quickly do we humble ourselves and confess our error? How quickly do we restore another's safety?

I can tell you, Ken was definitely not feeling safe for those few days, but once I was able to see how I was being and was able to apologize, his soul felt safer than ever before. He witnessed my commitment to him, to us, and to practicing Safe Souls to the best of my ability.

No one is perfect. There will be times when we fall into the unsafe zone. And it can often happen with those we love the most. Give yourself permission to be imperfect. But don't allow yourself to stay there for very long. Thich Nhat Hanh, the famous Vietnamese Buddhist monk, teacher, author, poet, and peace advocate teaches us that: *People deal too much with the negative, with what is wrong. Why not try and see positive things, to just touch those things and make them bloom.*

If not for the health and wellbeing of others, practice the Fourth Dimension for your own vitality. During her TEDx Wall Street talk, Dr. Pam Peeke reported, "We have a brand new science that says every single thought you have, every single mouthful you eat, and every single step you take changes your gene expression, changes the way your whole body talks to itself, and changes your destiny. That's right, you write your own life's script." We can literally alter our cell's very expression by our thoughts—will they become diseased or robust? She asked the audience, "What kinds of thoughts are you having? Positive thoughts? Loving thoughts? You're changing your very epigenome."

Epigenome: *a network of chemical compounds surrounding DNA that modify the genome without altering the DNA sequences and have a role in determining which genes are active in a particular cell.*

A few years ago, I had my DNA tested through 23andMe.com. Using a very simple and inexpensive saliva test, they screened for a host of health risks and genetic traits. I was mainly curious about Alzheimer's disease, as it runs on both sides of my family. The results indicated that I am almost twice as likely to contract Alzheimer's than the average Caucasian woman of my age with European decent. Yikes. This knowledge provides me with a very strong incentive to eat healthy foods, to stay physically active, to challenge my mind regularly, to maintain close relationships, and now, with this new epigenetic information, to monitor my thoughts diligently.

Practice Safe Souls not only in your *speaking*—make every attempt to practice Safe Souls in your *thinking*.

THE FIFTH DIMENSION

The Fifth Dimension includes gossiping about, triangulating with, or criticizing *ourselves*. And if you don't think one person can gossip or triangulate, you have not heard the committee in my head! Acknowledging and clearing our own thoughts is vital. We cannot give away what we do not have. We cannot be safe for others if we cannot be safe for ourselves and each time we judge ourselves we break our own heart. Not only do we do ourselves great harm, if we do not have self-love and acceptance, it is almost impossible to have it for others. Former American pro-surfer and fashion model, Laird Hamilton, reminds us, "Make sure your worst enemy doesn't live between your two ears." Have you considered the thoughts you think about yourself lately?

Light and dark cannot exist together simultaneously, and neither can negative and positive thoughts. Telling someone to just stop thinking negative thoughts is like telling someone to stop thinking about the pink elephant in the corner. Once someone mentions the pink elephant, you cannot un-think it. So instead of wasting energy trying to erase negative thoughts, try replacing them with positive ones. We can do this using Positive Affirmations.

I encourage you to take a journal and jot down the *opposite* of any GTC thoughts you have about yourself. Replace, "I'm being so freaking lazy," with, "I am a productive and active machine and taking some down time is essential!" Trade, "Why do I get frustrated?" with, "I live life peacefully and gracefully, even when surrounded by challenging people." Exchange, "I'm such a bad auntie," with, "I am a great auntie! My nieces and nephews love me and we've created some amazing memories together!" Get it?

Here are some simple and practical rules concerning affirmations:

1. Begin them with "*I statements*." This clearly states the intention is about you. This is programming your mind (especially your unconscious mind) to pay attention. This is really a process of reprogramming your thought patterns, so you have to be direct.

2. They should be *positive* statements, never negative ones. You are declaring an optimistic state of being, not something of which you want to rid yourself. Instead of saying, "I want to lose these stubborn ten pounds." You can say, "I commit to making healthy choices everyday." Or, "I lovingly release everything from my body that doesn't serve me." Both together would be ideal.

3. The statements should *exist right now*. It is telling your brain you already exist in a certain positive state so your actions, thoughts, behaviors, and motivations will grow from that place. Instead of saying, "I want to make a six figure income by the end of the year," you can say, "I am growing my financial wealth every day and in every way."

4. Say them *often*. Post them on your bathroom mirror so you see them when you wake up and when you go to bed. Post them on the dash of your car and on your computer. And say them aloud. Don't be shy, because declaring an affirmation aloud activates the brain as a command would. It becomes much more powerful than a benign thought.

The above are for the purpose of being a Safe Souls to yourself. To use affirmations to be a Safe Soul towards others, you can also post positive characteristics about people with whom you are having an inner (or outer) conflict. If there is someone at the office who continually hurts your feelings, or someone you find yourself thinking unsafe thoughts about, first try a Clearing Conversation. But if that does not resolve things, you can always try the positive affirmation route. Write down as many great things about that person as you can find. Post them where you will see them often. You might be surprised at how things change. In time, this practice may transform your thinking so much that you find yourself wanting to share your praises with the person.

I love the African proverb, "Beware of the naked man that offers you a shirt." We cannot be safe for others if we are not safe for ourselves. We cannot offer genuine love, if we do not harbor self-love. We often criticize ourselves more than we would our worst enemy. How would you describe a perceived enemy, an evil historical person, or a current public figure with which you would never want to spend one second? Then think about some of the thoughts you say about yourself? Similar? Close? Even in the same arena? They shouldn't be.

BURNING MAN

I recently attended a Burning Man festival in Nevada and I've never felt so 'safe' anywhere on the planet, nor with any other tribe of people. I think this was due to the *10 Burning Man Principles* that co-founder Larry Harvey wrote in 2004. They were not scribed as a dictate of how people should act, but rather as a reflection of the community's culture as it had organically grown since inception. The principles, as written on the official Burning Man website, and my thoughts regarding such, are as follows:

1. Radical Inclusion

Anyone may be a part of Burning Man. We welcome and respect the stranger. No prerequisites exist for participation in our community.

• Sounds pretty awesome, yes?

2. Gifting

Burning Man is devoted to acts of gift giving. The value of a gift is unconditional. Gifting does not contemplate a return or an exchange for something of equal value.

• How honored and safe do you feel when someone bestows an unconditional gift upon you?

3. Decommoditization

In order to preserve the spirit of gifting, our community seeks to create social environments that are unmediated by commercial sponsorships, transactions, or advertising. We stand ready to protect our culture from such exploitation. We resist the substitution of consumption for participatory experience.

- This forces real community, as there is no commercial aspect whatsoever. There are no purchasable commodities. If you need something you don't have in the moment, you have to ask someone for it, without the use of cash. Imagine that. I remember riding my bike along, feeling very thirsty. Normally, I would just whip into a store and purchase a drink. But in this case, I had to pull up to some unknown person's contribution and ask for refreshment. I had nothing to give back except my gratitude. It was a very odd feeling. When we create vulnerability by asking for something, trust somehow grows.

4. Radical Self-reliance

Burning Man encourages the individual to discover, exercise and rely on his or her inner resources.

- This leaves no room for people to use each other. Don't mistake not having a real need in a certain moment and asking for it to be met, with not being radically self-reliant. The two concepts are not mutually exclusive.

5. Radical Self-expression

Radical self-expression arises from the unique gifts of the individual. No one other than the individual or a collaborating group can determine its content. It is offered as a gift to others. In this spirit, the giver should respect the rights and liberties of the recipient.

- This, for me, is at the heart of Safe Souls. Live and let live. Better yet, live and celebrate the uniqueness of others.

6. Communal Effort

Our community values creative cooperation and collaboration. We strive to produce, promote and protect social networks, public spaces, works of art, and methods of communication that support such interaction.

- Sounds like a safe tribe, yes?

7. Civic Responsibility

We value civil society. Community members who organize events should assume responsibility for public welfare and endeavor to communicate civic responsibilities to participants. They must also assume responsibility for conducting events in accordance with local, state and federal laws.

- Keeping everyone physically safe is a clear and given aspect of Safe Souls.

8. Leaving No Trace

Our community respects the environment. We are committed to leaving no physical trace of our activities wherever we gather. We clean up after ourselves and endeavor, whenever possible, to leave such places in a better state than when we found them.

- This speaks to an uncommon and radical emphasis on respect. When a community operates with this level of reverence for the environment, I believe it spills over into a higher level of respect for its fellow man. Why wouldn't we also attempt to leave everyone's soul in a better state than we found it? Love, acceptance, and praise works wonders on this front.

9. Participation

Our community is committed to a radically participatory ethic. We believe that transformative change, whether in the individual or in society, can occur only through the medium of deeply personal participation. We achieve being through doing. Everyone is invited to work. Everyone is invited to play. We make the world real through actions that open the heart.

- This sounds like the cultivation of self-actualization, which is not possible if the more elementary levels of Maslow's Hierarchy of Needs are not being met. If we don't feel safe amid our fellow man, we cannot self-actualize. Social harmony also flourishes during a Burning Man celebration.

10. Immediacy

Immediate experience is, in many ways, the most important touchstone of value in our culture. We seek to overcome barriers that stand between us and a recognition of our inner selves, the reality of those around us, participation in society, and contact with a natural world exceeding human powers. No idea can substitute for this experience.[10]

- One is not likely to embrace this if one does not first feel safe. Since judgment and criticism are virtually nonexistent on the 'playa,' people are free to participate unencumbered as opportunities arise.

These are perfect principles to integrate into our daily lives. While many 'religious' people might view Burning Man as a pagan event, I do not see it that way. There certainly are aspects of the festival which I avoid as they do not align with my core values, but it is still a deeply spiritual event and extremely full of love—the very thing most religious or philosophical traditions preach. And I do not view 'my' core values as being the 'right' core values. They are simply what I know work for me in this moment of time, based on the experiences I've had. Someone else has had an entirely different set of experiences and his or her worldview will be adjusted accordingly. It is never mine to judge.

Google CEO, Larry Page says, "There are many, many exciting and important things we can do, but we can't do because they're illegal or not allowed by regulations," he said, adding that it might be good to designate an experimental zone reminiscent of the annual "Burning Man" art and technology festival where

---

10. http://blog.burningman.com/10principles/

many social rules are suspended. "As technologists, we should have safe places where we can try out new things and figure out the effect on society and people without having to deploy into the normal world. People who like those kind of things can go there and experiment."[11]

I find it interesting that he used the words 'safe place.' It is what we all crave.

Most every 'Burner' I met fell into the Safe Soul Zone. I heard no gossip, no triangulation, and no criticism. People were absolutely free to just be themselves. There were no sideways glances, no tsk-tsks, no rolling eyes, well…no judgment. People were radically free to be fully self-expressed. It was refreshing for my soul and I was deeply grateful.

My dream is that we don't need to spend a week in the hot and dusty desert to experience Safe Souls, but that we feel it everyday in our regular lives—be it in the schoolyard, the family room, the boardroom, or just hanging out with friends. I see a future for the planet where we are all fully self-expressed, without fearing that our souls will be hammered for it.

Exercise #6: Seven-Day Positivity Challenge

For the next seven days:

1. Do not speak negatively about anyone, anything, any place, or any situation. No GTC.

2. Practice the Fourth Dimension of Safe Souls. If we refrain from speaking negativity, but our minds are full of un-checked toxic thoughts, they will come out passive-aggressively. As outlined previously, the key here is to transform your thinking as this will transform your words, your actions, your habits, your character, and ultimately your destiny.

---

11. http://www.siliconbeat.com/2013/05/16/larry-page-holds-forth-on-technology-society-and-burning-man/

3. Adhere to the Fifth Dimension by ceasing all negative self-talk.

This will be quite a radical redirect for most people and the habit of GTC may crop up unexpectedly. Use SOAP immediately. Negative thoughts may arise, but simply practice mindful kindness to yourself and others by changing your thoughts to something more positive. I challenge you to note how different your energy levels feel during this exercise.

It is my sincere hope that taking up this challenge for one week—practicing No GTC plus adding in the Fourth and Fifth Dimensions—will be so transformational that you will take up the challenge for a lifetime. You will be operating at a level of such immense positivity, productivity, and personal power, that you will never want to go back. You will exude kindness, grace, safety, and trustworthiness.

TEN ACTIONABLE STEPS FOR CREATING SAFE SOULS

Are you ready to fully implement Safe Souls in your life today? If so, here are ten actions you can take to create immediate and life-long changes. These are only the first steps however, as Safe Souls is a living practice. It is meant to grow as you, your company, and the people with whom you surround yourself grow along with it.

1. Read this short book and, if necessary, read it twice. Ponder where you are on the safe to unsafe souls continuum in your business and personal relationships. Write down your thoughts. Do you feel safe in your relationships? Do you know when you walk away from someone that they have your back? Do you actively create safety in your relationships? Do you have other people's backs? Are you committed to transforming some or all of these relationships?

2. Make a list of all people in your circle of influence

with whom you are committed to creating a Safe Souls environment. Write beside each person's name anything you would like to clear up. This can include past ways you were unsafe to them or have felt unsafe in their presence. People who fear confrontation may have a hard time admitting there is anything in the space of a relationship, but if you sense something, take courage and discuss it. Create a safe place where that person can vent and discuss whatever is bothering her. It will be a gift.

3. Speak with each person regarding your commitment to practicing **No Gossip**. Differentiate gossip and *positive* gossip, give real life examples of each, and explain why and how to live without the former.

4. Speak with each person regarding your commitment to practicing **No Triangulation**. Take them through the distinction. Define triangulation, give real life examples, and explain why and how to refrain from it.

5. Speak with each person regarding your commitment to practicing **No Criticism** or personal judgment. Explain the difference between personal criticism and performance judgment, give real life examples of each, and explain why and how to avoid being critical.

6. Speak with each person regarding the **Tools for Transformation**. Take them through each of the four tools—Clearing Conversations, Committed Conversations for Action, Covering People's Backs, and Private/Public Praise. Define each, give examples, and explain why and how these practices are effective.

7. Describe the **Fourth Dimension** and the power of our thoughts. Give examples of transforming negative thinking towards others into positive thinking and praise.

8. Explain the **Fifth Dimension** and the importance of being a Safe Soul to ourselves. Would we accuse our worst enemy of the things which we often accuse ourselves?

9. Create existence systems to remind yourself about your commitment to practicing Safe Souls. Post notes in your car, your home, your office, and any other place they will be visual and helpful. Set up auto-emails reminding you to be kind, to THINK before you speak, and to use SOAP when you err. Ask a friend to keep you accountable. The more ideas you put into actual existence systems, the better your chance of creating kind, clean, and clear communication in all your relationships.

10. Interview your team members, friends, and family members on an ongoing basis regarding your commitment to refraining from gossiping, triangulating, and criticizing/personally judging others. Be open to their feedback and adjust accordingly. Also, check in with yourself regarding your success around practicing the Fourth and Fifth Dimensions.

After flexing your Safe Souls muscles, teaching those around you to do the same, and experiencing the fruit of this way of operating, you will have created a haven of peace and safety for yourself and those around you.

The Butterfly Effect is real. You will be amazed by the powerful shift your commitment to Safe Souls generates, even if it feels inconsequential initially. We know that most of humanity wants this. Religious and philosophical documentation has existed for many thousands of years, showing us that the principles Safe Souls espouses will produce peace. Especially in today's chaotic and often negative world, once we are aware, we will always gravitate toward those living these principles. The absence of love, kindness, and appreciation—for ourselves and for others—is fundamentally uncomfortable to our souls. We all need a soft place to land. We all want to feel safe.

Maybe we are closer to the ideal than we think. Maybe we can become the change we wish to see in the world quite easily. All groups of which we are members—friends, family, or business associates—will be more harmonious with Safe Souls in place.

It will help us grow in lightness and positivity and will diminish the heavy burden that negativity brings. When we get tangled up, we have a simple choice to make—do we stay ensnared or do we use the Safe Souls formula to guide us back to that place where we, and those around us, become free?

Mark Twain had it right when he said, "Kindness is the language which the deaf can hear and the blind can see." I believe kindness is an exquisite and loving safety net for everyone's soul. And safety is the gateway to self-actualization, social harmony, and ultimately peace on earth. Will you choose kindness? Will you be a Safe Soul?

CPSIA information can be obtained
at www.ICGtesting.com
Printed in the USA
LVOW04*2159140916

504660LV00009B/29/P